T
RAC
DRIVER'S
POCKET-BOOK

COMPILED BY
COLIN GOODWIN

CONWAY

A Conway book

Selection and introduction © Colin Goodwin 2011
Volume © Conway 2011

First published in 2011 by Conway,
An imprint of Anova Books Ltd.
10 Southcombe Street
London W14 0RA
www.anovabooks.com

A CIP record of this book is available from the British Library.

ISBN 9781844861347

Typesetting and origination by SX Composing DTP Ltd
Printed and bound by Bookwell, Finland

Permissions and image credits
Front cover: Detail from a poster for the Brooklands 'Double-Twelve Hour Race', designed by F. Gordon Crosby, c.1930 © Mary Evans Picture Library/Onslow Auctions Limited. p18, p25, p35, *p43 (top) and p57 © Getty Images. Images and text pp36-39 and pp42-59* reproduced with the kind permission of Haymarket Media Group. Text pp40-41 reproduced with the kind permission of *Motor Sport* magazine. 'Driving a Racing Car' taken from *Competition Driving* © Paul Frère 1963 (B. T. Batsford Ltd., 1963). 'Cars and Marques' drawings p108 and pp112–118 taken from *The British Competition Car* by Cyril Posthumus with drawings by John Dunscombe (B. T. Batsford Ltd., 1959); p109, p111 and pp119–122 taken from *The Racing Car: Development and Design* by C. Clutton, C. Posthumus and D. Jenkinson (B. T. Batsford Ltd., 1962).

CONTENTS

INTRODUCTION

The early days of motor racing

The love of speed and the desire to compete seems to be almost as natural to the human being as the need for water and oxygen. It is generally agreed among bicycle historians that the earliest patent for a pedal-powered bicycle was lodged in 1866. It didn't take long for someone to organise a race for them. It was held in Paris in 1868 and was won by an Englishman called James Moore.

Early in the 19th century, around the same time that bicycle inventors were hard at work, engineers were scratching their heads over the tricky problem of coming up with a motorised carriage. Designs had been around since the 17th century but it wasn't until Richard Trevithick wheeled out his *Puffing Devil* road locomotive in 1801 that the world saw the first working example of a self-propelled carriage. However, this steam-powered machine could not hold its pressure for long and was incredibly slow – not much good for racing, that's for sure. Indeed, for the most part of the 19th century inventors and engineers were having enough trouble making a vehicle that worked to worry about whether it would be faster than a rival machine. And then in 1886 there was a breakthrough when Karl Benz patented the first four-stroke internal combustion engine. Others were still fiddling about with steam engines and even electrically-powered cars. A revolution was taking place and in 1894 the inevitable happened: someone decided that there should be a race.

The course ran from Paris to Rouen and stretched for 80 miles. The winner was Albert de Dion, but unfortunately for the future motor manufacturer and inventor, he was not awarded a prize because his machine was steam powered and he had a stoker on board, which was deemed to have contravened the rules of the race. A year later a far more adventurous competition was staged, this time a massive 732-mile round trip, Paris–Bordeaux–Paris. Emile Levassor was the winner in his Panhard, driving for 48 hours at an average speed of 15mph. Also in the race was Edouard Michelin, who was giving the pneumatic tyre its racing debut. Despite Michelin finishing last and having suffered 22 punctures en route, within a couple of years virtually all racing machines were fitted with pneumatic tyres. Sadly, Emile Levassor would subsequently enter history as the first victim of the new sport of automobile racing, dying a year after he sustained serious injuries while competing in the Paris–Marseille–Paris race of 1896.

These new motor races didn't just draw in derring-do types that had either the money to develop these novel machines or buy those made by others, but also vast crowds of spectators – most of whom would have never seen a motor car 'in the metal', let alone seen one driven in anger flat out across dirt roads, by a succession of eccentrically dressed drivers and mechanics. The race routes were lined with crowds but the serious fan would want to be at the start of the event. Selwyn Edge, one of Britain's pioneer racers and a man we shall meet again shortly, competed in the 1899 Paris-Bordeaux race and described the start for a newspaper reporter:

'Pandemonium broke out; the engines of the unsilenced cars roared, motor tricyclists pedalled for dear life, cars ran onto the footpath, pedestrians and cyclists hurled themselves into places of safety. Several engines refused to fire, while others gave forth a half-hearted explosion or two and then stopped. Minor collisions were frequent.'

Edge touched on a key concern of early motor racing: 'Would the wretched engine start and if it did, how long would it continue to run?' In the early years of development of the internal combustion engine, reliability was the overriding issue. Not just because the designs were so new, but also because of the great demands placed on the metals used to manufacture the engine's component parts. The multitude of testing processes used today, including X-ray examination for cracks in crankshafts and connecting rods, did not exist in the late 19th and early 20th centuries. Metallurgy was a relatively new science and an increasingly important one.

Initially manufacturers were not primarily concerned with offering customers fast motor cars, but simply models that were reliable; cars able to actually complete a journey without breaking down. Of course reliability was often professed in advertising materials, but such claims could be disputed. What couldn't be contested was glory; triumph in one of the long distance races. After all, if a new motor car could cover 700 miles at speed, without serious mishap, then it could easily deliver her ladyship to the railway station. The great road races were a massive news event with all the important newspapers covering the event. A win would immediately put a new manufacturer on the map, guaranteeing instant credibility and, by extension, sales.

Modern-day Formula One racing teams, and especially the automotive manufacturers who sponsor such teams or supply them with engines proclaim that 'racing improves the breed' and that the lessons learned through grand prix testing and racing will eventually be incorporated into road cars available to the public. It is generally speaking pure marketing spin. Today's family saloon car contains far more complex systems than a contemporary racing car. Sophisticated stability control systems, intelligent cruise control, pedestrian awareness systems; all developed on road cars for road cars. This would not be the case if the technical rules in F1 were more open and perhaps one day they will be again. But in the early days of motor racing, the adage that 'racing improves the breed' was absolutely true. New inventions came thick and fast in the joint pursuit of speed and reliability.

One of the spectators at that first motor race from Paris to Rouen was a millionaire publishing tycoon called James Gordon Bennett. The son of an Irish immigrant, Bennett had a wild streak and a nose for good publicity. It was Bennett's paper that put up the cash for Henry Stanley's search for Dr Livingstone. But now Gordon Bennett spotted the publicity value of motor racing and became its first sponsor. He never competed himself or even drove a car on the road, but he put his company's wealth behind the International Trophy. Bennett wanted to publicise his newspapers but also had the more altruistic motive of wanting to create international competition between car makers to further the cause and development of the motor car.

The first Gordon Bennett International Trophy race was held in France on 14 June 1900. Rather than individuals competing, the Trophy was competed for by national teams, each nation entering three cars. Every part of the car had to be built in the country entering it and the drivers had to be a member of the respective country's national motoring club.

The 1900 race ran from Paris to Lyon, a distance of 353 miles and was won by French driver Fernand Charron. The American driver Alexander Winton retired after buckling a wheel, which led to one contemporary pundit commenting, with what to modern sensibilities seems like remarkable irony, that 'America has most things to learn in the craft of building a motor car'. France won again in 1901 but fortunately for British pride the 1902 event was won by our friend Selwyn Edge in a Napier.

Edge's win was also good news for the event itself, because after a disastrous race from Paris to Madrid in May 1903, in which eight people died and many more were injured (including spectators), motor racing on public roads in France was banned. As Edge was British and then the holder of the Trophy, it seemed fitting that the 1903 race should be held in Britain. Unfortunately, Britain wasn't the ideal venue for a motor race. Firstly, there was a rigidly enforced speed limit; second, no purpose-built race track and lastly, a public that was overwhelmingly hostile to the motor car. A most embarrassing situation, but fortunately the secretary of the Automobile Club of Great Britain, a lateral thinker called Claude Johnson, had the bright idea of suggesting that Ireland host the race. Which is exactly what happened. The British team painted their Napier cars in Shamrock green as a thank-you to their Irish friends for hosting the race. Edge was defending the Trophy, but the race was won by Belgian Camille Jenatzy driving a Mercedes.

Brooklands, racing, flying and the Great War

War in the 20th century was a catalyst for technological advance, which proceeded at a rate never seen in peacetime. The demands of the Great War, particularly in aviation, accelerated engine development and the advancement of engineering processes and materials at a terrific pace. Motor racing is the other great contributor to technical progress, but in war research and development is funded by government – when winning really is a matter of life and death.

In Britain, the worlds of motor racing and aviation famously came together at the Brooklands racing circuit and aerodrome in Weybridge, Surrey. That same blanket 20mph speed limit that caused the 1903 Gordon Bennett Trophy to be held in Ireland was holding back car development in Britain. At that time around half of the world's cars were built in France and more than a few patriots in this country were worried that Blighty was being seriously left behind. It's hard to build and test world-beating cars with a 20mph speed limit.

Once such patriot was Hugh Locke-King, who built a high-speed test track and racing circuit on family-owned land at Brooklands. Opening in 1907, the banked Brooklands circuit was the first purpose-built racing circuit in the world. Paved in concrete, because laying Tarmacadam on a slope was too difficult and asphalt too expensive, the track was 2.75 miles long. At its peak 275,000 spectators could watch the racing.

The first section of this pocket book includes an amazing account of the first Brooklands meeting, held in June 1907, and originally published in the 9 July issue of the weekly motoring magazine *The Motor*. *The Motor* was first published in 1902, and along with *The Autocar* (which pre-dates its rival as the first English-language motoring magazine, first appearing in November 1895), was essential reading for the motoring enthusiast. Both of these magazines provide a fascinating eyewitness account of the development of racing and the remarkable achievements of the pioneering drivers.

The inter-war years

Out of the dreadful carnage of the Great War came a generation of young men relieved to have got through the conflict in one piece and determined that henceforth the life spared would be fully lived. The jazz age was coming, and with it a desire for excitement and challenge. Motor racing had been dangerous from the outset, as the Paris-Madrid and other early races had shown, but if you'd survived the artillery shells of the Somme or overcome the terrible odds dogfighting in the skies above, then perhaps racing at Brooklands didn't seem all that dangerous.

Today the organisers of motor racing are forever trying to keep costs down in all forms of racing. There is an image that in earlier times racing was inexpensive and open to all. It is a false one. The young men who started racing in the 1920s were wealthy, officer-class types and aristocrats. Men like Captain George Eyston. Eyston was born in 1897 and raced motorcycles under an assumed name while still a schoolboy. After distinguished service in the army during the war, in which he was awarded the Military Cross, Eyston took up racing again, though this time using his own name and competing in cars.

Eyston had numerous successes, usually in Aston Martins, before turning his hand to speed record breaking. A British driver winning a big race on the continent of course stirred national pride, but nothing gripped the public more strongly than the Land Speed Record being taken in the country's name. Throughout the 1920s and '30s Britain and America skirmished on race tracks, beaches and dry lake beds to try and become the fastest men on earth. The speeds reached were quite amazing. America's Tommy Milton took his Duesenberg to 156.047mph on Daytona Beach in 1920, less than twenty years after the first racing cars struggled to make half that speed. And the speeds continued to rise as the records fell. Drivers like Sir Malcolm Campbell were household names. Campbell was profiled in *Motor Sport* magazine (formerly known as the *Brooklands Gazette*) in 1932; again, this piece is included in this pocket book.

We have already met James Gordon Bennett, the world's first sponsor of a motor race. Sponsorship as we know it via today's motor racing did not exist until the mid 1960s, but although company names weren't emblazoned on the noses of racing cars in the inter-war years, commercial assistance was often provided. For example, a speed record attempt might be supported by an oil company, a tyre manufacturer or a maker of spark plugs. And as will be seen from period advertisements, if a car broke a record then Castrol were not shy about proclaiming the fact. It made excellent publicity – naturally, if Castrol oil could take Sir Malcolm Campbell or Henry Segrave to 200mph, it could certainly take the family to visit Auntie Gwen in Bridlington.

So far we have mentioned Levassor, Edge, Campbell and Segrave. More great racers followed, but before we go further we should meet a few other stars of the

1920s and '30s, who were equally remarkable – perhaps more so. Like the men, to race in those days one had to have money, but even with disposable funds, it must have been incredibly difficult for a girl to break into what even today remains a very male-dominated world. Even more remarkable if, like Kay Petre, you are only 4ft 10in in stature. Petre, an American by birth but married to an English aviator, was idolised by the public and was one of the biggest crowd draws at Brooklands. And she wasn't driving a light voiturette capable of modest speeds, either. She drove leviathans like the 10.5-litre V12 Delage, a machine in which, in 1934, she lapped the Brooklands outer circuit at an average speed of 129.58mph. This set the women's outer lap record, for which Petre fought with rival Gwenda Stewart repeatedly over the next few years (Stewart eventually managed 135.95mph in a custom-built Derby-Miller single-seater, which still survives today).

The Grand Prix

Modern motor racing is highly structured, consisting of various tiers of championships and classes, at the summit of which, of course, is Formula One. The sport was very different between the wars. In 1904 motoring clubs in Europe joined together to form the Association Internationale des Automobile Clubs Reconnus (AIACR) and in 1922 an offshoot called the Commission Sportive Internationale (CSI) was set up, leaving the AIACR to deal with touring and other motoring concerns. National clubs, such as the Royal Automobile Club in Britain, took charge of organising domestic racing while the CSI concentrated on the most important international races: the Grands Prix.

The first motor race to be called a 'Grand Prix' had been held in Pau, France in 1901. A regular French Grand Prix at Le Mans followed but it wasn't until 1921 that an Italian Grand Prix was held at Brescia. Belgium and Spain followed in 1924 and Great Britain in 1926 – the latter race of course, was held at Brooklands. As in modern day Grand Prix racing the rules that governed engine size and vehicle class were frequently changed, but in 1928 the rule book was practically thrown away as a new formula called Formula Libre was introduced. It was a new and exciting class of racing that was literally governed as the translation implies; a free formula with barely any technical constraints.

Grand Prix races grew in popularity and prestige, and the number of events per year increased steadily. In 1927 only five races were designated with Grand Prix status; by 1929 there were nine and in 1934 there were eighteen. As the number of races multiplied so too did the different marques and types of machines that entered them.

Delage, Bugatti, Alfa Romeo and the Silver Arrows

Given the roots of competitive motorsport in France, it is perhaps unsurprising that the same country had a prodigious output of racing cars as well as cars manufactured for the public. The French automobile marques, led by Bugatti and joined by Delage and Delahaye, dominated the early days of racing right up until the late 1920s. They'd had it relatively easy, but now the Italians arrived on the scene with their Alfa Romeos and Maseratis. Enzo Ferrari, who after the Second War started building his own racing machines, drove for Alfa Romeo in the 1920s and finished 2nd in the famous Targa Florio road race in Sicily driving a 4.5-litre Alfa 20/30 ES. Eventually Ferrari started a team called Scuderia Ferrari that ran the Alfas on behalf of the factory, an arrangement that came to an end in 1938 when Alfa Romeo decided to bring its racing cars back into the fold as a fully-fledged factory team. The company wanted to make a dedicated effort to take on two rival manufacturers that in the 1930s, particularly in the lead-up to the Second World War War, virtually dominated Grand Prix racing: the twin German marques Mercedes-Benz and Auto Union.

In 1934 the CSI introduced a maximum weight limit of 750kg. German manufacturer Auto Union (the company that eventually became the automotive conglomerate Audi) had decided to enter Grands Prix and had built a car designed specifically to compete under the new rules. The car was called the A-type and was powered by a 4.4-litre supercharged V16 engine placed behind the driver. The A-type was a highly advanced racer with a five-speed gearbox and a supercharged piston engine that generated 295bhp.

Mercedes-Benz also had a car for the new formula, called the W25. It wasn't as radical in design as the Auto Union but was powered by an eight-cylinder engine with 345bhp, mounted in the front of the car. Like the Auto Union cars, the Mercedes-Benz races were unpainted and raced in bare aluminium. The press soon christened these awesome and virtually unbeatable machines the *silberpfeil*, or Silver Arrows. These machines departed from Germany's traditional national racing colour of white, as both teams were desperate to save weight, supposedly shedding even the minimal additional ounces that a coat of white paint would cost.

The story of the Silver Arrows has continued to fascinate racing fans. With power outputs rising to over 600bhp (it wasn't until the 1980s that Grand Prix cars bettered that figure) the Auto Union and Mercedes-Benz were both incredible to watch and extremely challenging to drive. Their drivers became heroes; men like Bernd Rosemeyer and Hans Stuck in the Auto Unions and Manfred Von Brauchitsch and

Rudolf Carraciola driving for Mercedes. Mercedes-Benz had another driver on their roster, too – the dashing and talented Englishman Richard Seaman. And now we come to another reason why the story of the Silver Arrows continues to fascinate. The German Nazi government was determined that the country's two teams should show the world the might of German engineering and to that end provided financial support to both teams. As a result, the cars carried swastikas on their unpainted flanks. The irony of the English driver Richard Seaman driving cars in 1939 that wore the infamous symbol of the Nazi regime has never been lost. Tragically, Seaman was to die at the wheel of his Mercedes at the Belgian Grand Prix at Spa early in the 1939 season. The Spa circuit, nestled in the Ardennes forest near the German border, was one of racing's most terrifying circuits. Details of its layout and history, and that of other world-famous circuits, are featured in the final section of the book.

The Second World War

Obviously there was no motor racing from the start of war in September 1939 to the end of hostilities in Europe in May 1945. At least, one would assume that to be the case, but in fact the Tripoli Grand Prix was run in 1940 in the Italian colony that from 1934 had been known as Libya. Only the factory Alfa Romeo and Maserati teams took part so Giuseppe Farina's win in the Alfa 158 was a pyrrhic victory.

But despite the Blitz, rationing and the fact that a large percentage of Britain's youth were involved in the war, *Motor Sport* did not cease publication. Yes, the nation was at war, but that didn't necessarily mean that people discarded their hobbies and enthusiasms, or even put them on hold. As well as the shortage of paper and rationing of fuel, finding stories was a problem, but the magazine's dedicated small staff still managed to fill the admittedly rather thin publication with features on racing, car preparation, interviews with famous drivers and, best of all, thoughts about racing when the war was over.

Post-war racing and the birth of Formula One

Post-war Europe was slow to recover from the devastation of a shattering conflict, but as national governments set about rebuilding ruined cities and repairing infrastructure, racing enthusiasts were eager to get back to competition. It didn't take them long and predictably the French were the first to start racing again. Britain was now covered in airfields and aerodromes, usually sited in areas where noise was not a problem. Such locations typically featured a handy perimeter track, which once provided a taxiway for heavy bombers but now made the perfect racing track. Accordingly, the British Racing Drivers Club surveyed dozens of airfields, ultimately choosing the former Wellington bomber Operation Training Unit airfield at Silverstone in Northamptonshire as a suitable site for the preparation of a 3.67-mile circuit. This was duly laid out ready for the 1948 British Grand Prix, an event won by Luigi Villoresi in car #18, a Maserati 4CLT. Another driver didn't have quite such a good day as his Cooper broke down during the Grand Prix's supporting event, a race for 500cc cars. That driver was Stirling Moss, then only in his second year of racing but about to burst onto the scene in spectacular fashion.

In 1947 the AIACR renamed itself the Federation Internationale de l'Automobile, or the FIA for short. One of the FIA's first acts was to simplify the racing classes by putting Grand Prix cars into Formula One, and racers that had formerly been known as voiturettes (cars like the British ERA) into Formula Two. Similarly, Stirling Moss's 500cc Cooper was classified as a member of the new Formula Three series. Following the FIA's introduction of the Formula One championship, Guiseppe Farina, who we may remember from his meaningless win at the Tripoli Grand Prix in 1940, now had his day by becoming the first F1 world champion – still driving, as in 1940, for Alfa Romeo.

The technique of driving a racing car. Quickly

For many the most interesting and informative section of the *Racing Driver's Pocket Book* will relate to the practical aspects of the sport. The technique and physics of driving a racing car around a circuit have not changed over the decades. The same principles that enabled men like Lang and Carraciola to tame their ferocious Silver Arrows and beat their rivals are as relevant to those who dream of lining up on the grid with Jenson Button and Lewis Hamilton. Or indeed, for any enthusiast who wants to take part in trackdays or club racing.

Right from the start of racing and racing journalism, successful drivers have passed on their knowledge through features in motoring magazines and the publication of books. Paul Frere, one of the greatest motoring journalists ever and a winner at the famous Le Mans 24 hour race in a Ferrari, was perfectly equipped to write what is still a bible for aspiring racers. Published in 1963 and reprinted many times, Frere's *Competition Driving* takes us through all the techniques and explains the physics of driving a high performance car on the circuit. It makes great reading even for armchair fans who never intend to race at Silverstone or on any racing circuit.

The circuits

On the subject of circuits, no pocket book would be complete without a look at the great racing tracks. The early racing circuits presented a formidable challenge, as the concept of run-off areas and trackside safety was virtually alien. In Britain many circuits were sited at ex-RAF airfields, as has already mentioned. America's famous Indianapolis 'brickyard', on the other hand, was a purpose built speedbowl – not unlike Brooklands, but designed with a more symmetrical series of banked curves. Italy, too, had a banked circuit at Monza, while Germany had AVUS and France Montlhéry. In contrast, some of the greatest challenges were thrown down by circuits that for 364 days of the year were public roads. Today only Monaco and (part of) the Le Mans circuit survive – both still highlights of the motorsport calendar – but at one time France had many more. Reims, Rouen and Clermont Ferrand are the best known.

History best remembers, however, the great Italian road races. The oldest, the Targa Florio, used Sicilian roads from 1906 to the last true race in 1973, when it was decided that cars were just too fast – that same year former racing driver Helmut Marko had branded the race 'totally insane'. The other great Italian epic was the thousand-mile long Mille Miglia, an event that ran from Brescia to Rome and then back to Brescia. The race was held from 1927 to 1957 when it too was deemed too dangerous and was discontinued. The most famous of all Mille Miglia victories was that of Moss and Jenkinson in 1955, driving a Mercedes-Benz 300 SLR at an average speed of 100mph. The car, the feat and the driver were all celebrated – but the co-driver, Denis Jenkinson, is also fondly remembered. 'Jenks', a legendary motoring journalist, aided Moss with a detailed set of previously taken course notes written on a roller map housed in a metal alloy and perspex case – the first recorded example of the pace notes that are used in modern rallying.

I hope that this little pocket book will be similarly useful – a handy guide to the first great age of the racing driver.

Colin Goodwin, 2011

EARLY RACING

THE GORDON-BENNETT RACE OF 1903
HELD AT ATHY, IRELAND ON THE 2ND JULY 1903
WITH A DISTANCE OF 527.040 KM

BY JULIAN W. ORDE (Club Secretary, Automobile Club of Great Britain and Ireland)

ACCORDING to the rules of the Gordon-Bennett Cup, the race must take place in the country of the club holding the trophy, or in France if a suitable course be not available.

As the Automobile Club of Great Britain and Ireland, represented by Selwyn Edge on a Napier car, won the Cup in 1902, it became necessary that the race for 1903 should be held either in the British Isles or in France. After considering many suggestions, it was decided to hold the race in Ireland, provided the necessary authorisation to do so could be obtained from Parliament.

The Club contemplated organising an automobile tour through Ireland after the race, and particulars of the proposed course and of the subsequent tour were sent to a large number of influential persons and to some six hundred newspapers. The draft proposals were also laid before lieutenants of the Irish Counties, the County Councils, Borough Councils, Urban District Councils, Town Commissioners, &c. The attention of hotel proprietors and of the various railway and steamship companies was drawn to the great advantages which would accrue to Irish trade if the Gordon-Bennett race could be held in that country. Numerous favourable replies were received to these communications and also promises of support.

Resolutions in favour of holding the race were passed by the County Councils throughout Ireland, and later a monster petition was signed by all classes and presented to Parliament in favour of a special Bill being passed to empower the Irish authorities to close the public roads over which it was proposed to run the race.

On February 24 the first reading of the Bill was moved by Mr. John Scott Montagu in the House of Commons, and with the exception of a trivial hitch it went through all stages very rapidly. In the House of Lords the Bill was entrusted to Lord Londonderry, and it was passed by the Upper House also without delay.

The route chosen for the race passed through the counties of Kildare, Queens, and Carlow. The complete circuit measured 103 miles, and roughly speaking, it ran in the shape of the figure 8. To provide for the public safety was a matter of grave consideration, the importance of which was brought vividly forward by the ghastly failure of the Paris-Madrid automobile race during May.

After conferring with the Committee of the Club the Local Government Board of Ireland issued a set of very complete regulations. In order that the public might be fully warned of the dangerous consequences of encroaching upon the road during the race, notices were posted in conspicuous positions all along the route and in the adjoining market towns. The local inhabitants were also circularised and requested to co-operate with the organisers of the event in guarding against accidents.

To ensure safety to the spectators as well as to the drivers over such a long course, a large force of police under the command of the inspector-general of the Royal Irish Constabulary, Colonel Sir Neville Chamberlain, K.C.B., were present, and some two thousand soldiers forming the camp at the Curragh were on duty under the command of Major-General Sir G. de C. Morton, K.C.I.E., C.V.O., C.B.

Many willing volunteers, members of the Club and others, gave their services as road stewards and performed invaluable services in the 'controls' and at various other points of the route. A large number of motor cyclists also rendered assistance as despatch-riders; they were divided into separate corps under captains, and were stationed at all important points. Their duties were often laborious, for in conveying their despatches they had to traverse bye-roads with which many of them were quite unacquainted.

Wire fences were erected across all roads converging upon the course (numbering about 270), in order that no stray cattle or horses could by any possible chance wander into the highway and so endanger the life of the competitors. Where possible, motor-cars belonging to members of the Club were also drawn up across the converging roads as an additional precaution.

The four competing Clubs were represented as follows:-

* The A.C.G.B. & I.: Three Napier cars, driven by Messrs. Selwyn Edge, Charles Jarrott, and J. W. Stocks.

* The A.C. of France: Two Panhards and one Mors car, driven

respectively by the Chevalier Rene de Knyff, Henri Farman, and Gabriel.

* The A.C. of America: Two Winton and one Peerless cars, driven by Messrs. Alexander Winton, Percy Owen, and L. P. Mooers.

* The A.C. of Germany: Three Mercedes cars, driven by Baron de Caters, Foxhall Keene, and Camille Jenatzy.

On the day before the race, namely July 1, the twelve competing cars were inspected and weighed at the town of Naas, the county town of Kildare. Several of the cars were found to be over the weight limit of 1,000 kilograms (or just under one ton), and these had to be stripped of everything not absolutely essential, in order to bring them within the regulation. It was a curious sight to see to what straits some of the competitors were brought in endeavouring to reduce the weight of their vehicles, every minute particle of unnecessary material being removed in the process.

The race was run on July 2, 1903, and thanks to the Local Government Board's regulations, the roads were, on that day, to all intents and purposes the private property of the A.C.G.B. & I.

The order of starting had been arranged as follows:—

* A.C.G.B. & I.: ... (1) Edge. ... (5) Jarrott. ... (9) Stocks.

* A.C. of France: ... (2) De Knyff. ...

(6) Gabriel. ... 10) Farman.

* A.C. of America: ... (3) Owen. ...

(7) Mooers. ... (11) Winton.

* A.C. of Germany: ... (4) Jenatzy. ...

(8) De Caters. ... (12) Keene.

Before the race started, two pilot cars were sent round the course as a warning that the racers would follow shortly, but by a mistake they both followed the western circuit and thus the eastern circuit did not know that the race had begun until the actual competitors appeared. Selwyn Edge was started off at 7 A.M., and the others followed at intervals of seven minutes. In order that very high rates of speed should be avoided in populous places where danger might be expected, nine controls were established on the course. Upon reaching a control each car had to stop and proceed over a measured portion of the road at a low speed, an allowance being made in the final reckoning for the time thus lost.

The eventual result of the race is given opposite.

It will be noticed that in the first time round, the Napier car covered the eastern, or shorter, circuit in the fastest time, and that the Mors car covered the western, or longer, circuit in the first round in less time than any of the other vehicles; but the great consistency with which the winning car accomplished the circle of the western circuit is also worthy of note.

Mr. Winton, who started eleventh, was in trouble at once, through the choking of the spray tube of his carburetter, and was delayed for about an hour at the starting-point.

The English competitors were remarkably unfortunate. Stocks on his first round over the eastern circuit met with an accident through mistaking the road, his car ran into one of the wire fences previously mentioned which became so entangled with the vehicle that it was too damaged to continue, and thus Stocks was early out of the race. Jarrott unluckily came to grief through his steering-gear snapping and causing the car to turn over, but fortunately he escaped serious injury.

When this mishap took place, wild rumours spread around the course to the effect that a terrible smash-up had occurred.

It was at this point that Baron de Caters behaved in such a chivalrous manner. Knowing that the spectators on the Club grand stand would be feeling anxious about Jarrott, he actually stopped his car to state that although the vehicle was smashed the driver was not seriously injured. When one considers the keen excitement of the race and realises the importance of every second lost, the sportsmanlike action of Baron de Caters can be appreciated. These unfortunate accidents left England with only one representative at a comparatively early stage.

Edge was, however, also in difficulties, as will be seen by reference to the times of the several cars quoted above, the chief trouble apparently being the difficulty of keeping the tyres on the back wheels of the car, owing to the enormous power developed and the

CONTESTANTS.	RESULTS
1. Selwyn Edge. Napier.	9h 18m 48s (disqualified for a push-start)
2. Rene de Knyff. Panhard.	Finished 2nd in 6h 50m 40s
3. Percy Owen. Winton.	Did not finish.
4. Camille Jenatzy. Mercedes.	Finished 1st in 6h 39m 00s
5. Charles Jarrott. Napier.	Did not finish.
6. Fernand Gabriel. Mors Z.	Finished 4th in 7h 11m 33s
7. Louis Mooers. Peerless.	Did not finish.
8. Pierre de Caters. Mercedes.	Did not finish.
9. J. Stocks. Napier.	Did not finish.
10. Henry Farman. Panhard.	Finished 3rd in 6h 51m 44s
11. Alexander Winton. Winton.	Did not finish.
12. Foxhall Keene. Mercedes.	Did not finish.

Camille Jenatzy drives his Mercedes to victory for Germany in the 1903 Gordon Bennett race at Athy, in Ireland. Jenatzy completed the 327 miles in 6 hours 39 minutes, winning by over 11 minutes.

high speed at which it travelled. Later, a Mercedes car, driven by Foxhall Keene, had to retire on account of the rear axle breaking, and for a similar cause the car driven by Baron de Caters had subsequently to be withdrawn.

The American cars made a very poor show, and went out one by one at various stages. It is safe to say that the industry is in its infancy in the United States, at all events as far as racing machines are concerned. As a result of the race the competitors must have realised that a car, the highest speed of which is fifty miles per hour on the level, is of no use for the purpose of a long road race; for it is obvious that a much

higher speed is necessary in order even to remain in the running. One of the strongest points in connection with the Mercedes cars which told so much in their favour was the ease with which they could be started, and the smooth manner in which the gears worked.

The Lord-Lieutenant of Ireland, the Earl of Dudley, took considerable interest in the arrangements for the race, and did a great deal towards the successful carrying out of the proposal for it to be run in Ireland; and there can be no doubt that it did much good for the country, for many thousand pounds were spent there which otherwise would probably have been spent in France.

BROOKLANDS.

Successful inaugural meeting. Large attendance. Fast races, but no times. Exciting dead heat.

The quietude of the fir-clad slopes at Weybridge was disturbed on Saturday by the roar and rattle of open exhausts. A party rusticating out of sight of the Brooklands enclosure might have imagined that a hundred Gatling guns were operating in the vicinity. So much for the sounds that assailed the hearing of anybody within a radius of five miles. The sights that met the gaze in the 'paddock' were equally striking and even more unusual. Strange contrasts were presented when great cars, belching forth clouds of smoke and handled by greasy drivers, lined up for inspection, and were surrounded by fashionably-attired ladies and gentlemen. The first great meeting at the Brooklands motor racing track was in progress. On the slopes overlooking the long, wide finishing straight there was an animated crowd. Fashion and beauty were present, and the high banks presented a picture of animation and colour. The attention of society was for the moment diverted from the turf and the paddock, as generally understood, to the

"PADDOCK" OF THE NEW ORDER

and the great cement course sweeping and curving around the expanse of country like an unrolled ribbon, and rolling up in a wide, straight line to the feet of the onlookers on the stands. As a spectacle the first Brooklands meeting was unique. But of all places at the new track the "paddock" of the new order was the most interesting. Here the "tuning up" was taking place. Here the weighing in was being conducted with order and method pleasant and interesting to watch. Here the racing monsters gave the onlooker a foretaste of their own mighty power, and of the power and ease with which the grim individuals grasped the steering wheels could manipulate and control the vehicles. The novelty of the whole thing was unique, because here and here alone could such sights be seen. Brooklands is unique.

The meeting was a first effort, and it is safe to assume that, as the authorities settle down to their work, many improvements will be introduced. It would be idle to deny that the meeting did not reveal defects. Generally speaking, the Press is not exacting. Under conditions such as those prevailing on Saturday, however, a system of communications between authorities and Pressmen was obviously necessary to ensure some measure of accuracy. If errors of reporting have been made in the general press, the management are more responsible that the representatives of the Press. We are not complaining on our own account, because our resources were sufficient to ensure the obtaining of reliable information on the spot. But inattention to the needs of the average reporter will, if persisted in, lead to errors which will misguide the public and be harmful to the sport. Authoritative information should, under prevailing conditions, be handed to the Press. The failing on Saturday was that the cars were not sufficiently distinctive. The numbering of the competing cars was a mere haphazard device, numbers being put on anyhow and anywhere. In fact, for purposes of identification on cars travelling at high speed the numbers were quite useless. In the report of the racing which follows the information concerning the happenings to the various cars is gathered from interviews with drivers and from our personal inspection of the cars on their arrival in the paddock. We have every reason, therefore, to believe that our information is correct. We have to thank no single official for the slightest inkling of authoritative information, and we have reason to believe that every Pressman on the ground was left to draw his own

conclusions according to his own devices.

Speaking generally, the inaugural meeting was a distinct success. We had representatives in the paddock, in the 5s. enclosure, and in the grandstand. Their impressions follow the report.

The Racing.

The officials of the meeting were as follows:—

STEWARDS.—Col. H. C. L. Holden, the Earl of Dudley, and the Earl of Lonsdale.

JUDGE.—Mr. A. S. Manning.

STARTER.—Mr. H. Owen.

CLERK OF THE SCALES.—Mr. W. E. Bushby.

CIRCUIT COUNTER.—Mr. A. V. Ebblewhite.

CLERK OF THE COURSE and RACING MANAGER.—Mr. E. de Rodakowski.

First race (run in two heats and a final). Distance 11.4328 miles. The Marcel Renault Memorial Plate of 550sov. for motorcars with a cylinder dimension 85 to under 110, weight 3,000lb.

First heat : Mr. S. F. Edge's Napier (3,009lb.), driven by Mr. H. C. Tryon, first. Mr. A. Huntley Walker's Darracq (3,052lb.), owner driving, second. Mr. P. Kerr-Smiley's Renault (3,202lb.), driver Mr. J. Groves, third.

Second heat : Capt. G. Ll. Hindes Howell's Iris (3,013lb.), driver Mr. A.

Clifford Earp, first. Mr. F. R .S . Bircham's Iris (3,049lb.), owner driving, second. Mr. H. R. Pope's Itala (3,140 lb.), third.

Final heat : S. F. Edge's Napier, first. Capt. G. Ll. Hindes Howell's Iris, seond. Mr. Huntley Walker's Darracq, third. The

RACE WAS NEVER IN DOUBT,

the Napier going off with the lead. Once it looked as if the Iris was gaining slightly, but Napier went away and won easily.

Second race. Distance 3.27995 miles. The Horsley Plate of 300sov. For motorcars with engines of cylinder dimensions of 60 to under 85 (3,000lb.), Mr. A Huntley Walker's Darracq (3,000lb.), driven by owner, first. Mr. Signey Straker's Straker-Squire (3,002lb.), driven by Mr. W. T. Lord, second. Mr. S. Gore-Brown's Thornycroft (3,000lb.), driven by owner, third. The Itala was the non-starter. Mr. Moss's Arrol-Johnston twice stopped her engines before going to the post. The Darracq led at the start, and won easily.

Third race. Distance 15.743 miles. The Gottlieb Daimler Memorial Plate of 650sov. For cars with engine of cylinder dimension 120 to 155. Weight 3,000lb. Mr. E. M. C. Instone's Daimler (3,083lb.), driven by owner, first. Mr. A.

Huntley Walker's Darracq (3,395lb.), second. Others tailed off. In this race the Minerva went away at a great rate, and led for three rounds, when a valve broke and it retired. Mr. Instone's Daimler then went ahead, and was never dispossessed of the lead. Whilst travelling at high speed the bonnet of Mr. Sangster's Ariel-Simplex flew open, and was seen flapping in the breeze. Mr. Sangster immediately received a copious flood of oil from the engine full in his face. This obscured his view, and he had to put up his goggles, only to receive

A BLINDING STREAM OF OIL FULL IN HIS UNCOVERED FACE.

Obviously he could not continue. His condition on returning to the paddock was a study, his face being absolutely smothered with engine oil. The Napier car was forced to retire through its water giving out, it being discovered that, after draining water away for weighing in, a water connection has not been properly re-fastened.

Fourth race. Distance 10.3078 miles. The Byfleet plate of 550sov. For motorcars having engines of a cylinder dimension 110 to under 135. Weight 3,000lb. Mr. C. Jarrott's Lorraine-Dietrich, driven by owner, and Mr. S. F. Edge's Napier (3,010lb.), driver

Mr. F. Newton, dead heat. Mr. Huntley Walker's Darracq (3,365lb.), third. A wonderfully quick change of valve was made in the Minerva, and it started in this race. This was the most exciting race of the day. Mr Jarrott's Lorraine-Dietrich went off with the lead, and held it for the first round. During the second circuit the Napier got on terms, and the two cars ran bonnet to bonnet for some time. Then the Dietrich gained again, and the two cars entered the last round locked together, the Dietrich seeming to be slightly ahead. Thus they entered the finishing straight, and the

RARE SIGHT OF A MAGNIFICENT TUSSLE

right to the tape was witnessed, the Napier sprinting up level, and the two cars going over the line together, the verdict being a dead-heat. Wagner, the famous Fiat driver, drove Mr. D'Arcy Baker's Fiat in this race.

Fifth race. Distance 30.456206 miles. The First Montagu Cup of 2,100 sov. For motorcars with engines of a cylinder dimension 155 to under 235. Weight 2,600lb. There were two non-starters. Baron Turckheim's Lorraine-Dietrich, which was to have been driven by Duray, and Mr. D'Arcy Baker's Fiat, which was to have been driven by Nazzaro.

Result: Mr. J. E. Hutton's Mercédès (2,726 lb.), driven by owner, first. Mr. K. Okura's Fiat (2,740 lb.), driven by owner, second. Mr. F. R. Fry's Mercédès (2,864 lb.), driver D. Resta, third. The race was marred by an unfortunate mishap to the Darracq driven by Warwick Wright.

He had exceedingly hard luck in this race, as he held a very long lead of the rest of the competitors in the last lap. We clocked him for several laps, which were run at a regular pace varying from 1min. 4⅘ sec. to 1min. 46sec., roughly about 91 to 94 miles per hour. We had it from Mr. Wright's own lips that the breakdown was due to a valve stem seizing (that must have occurred simultaneously with the firing point on one of the pistons), and, everything being suddenly jammed, one of the connecting rods was forced through the base chamber.

D. Resta, on Mr. Fry's Mercédès, assumed the lead, and should have won, but he went a circuit too many; through glancing at his burst rear tyre he missed the finishing signal at the fork. The Napier led in the first round, but after being passed by the Darracq retired in the fifth round through the water again giving out. The Mercédès driven by D. Resta finished with a burst tyre.

Sixth race. Distance 5.997 miles. The Stephenson Plate of 300 sov. for motorcars of a price not less than £600 and not exceeding £700. Weight 3,500 lb.

Mr. Huntley Walker's Darracq

(3,520 lb.), driver the Marquis de Mouzilly de St. Mars, first. Mr. Chas. Sangster's Ariel-Simplex (3,534 lb.), driver Mr. A. E. Harrison, second. Capt. W. E. D. Owen's Junior (3,500 lb.), driven by owner, third.

No times were recorded, and thus, in our opinion, the racing was robbed of much of its interest. Many well-known people were present, including Lord Lonsdale, Lord Caernarvon, the Duke of Westminster, Lord Montagu, Lord Essex, Lord Sefton, Lord Lovat, Lord Dalmeny, the Hon. A. Stanley M.P., Mr. C. D. Rose, M.P., Sir Thomas Lipton, Sir John Thornycroft, Mr. Lionel de Rothschild.

We are able to give the official returns of attendance, obtained from the Club, as we go to press: Public 11,000 + members and friends admitted on special vouchers, 2,500 = 13,500. In the enclosure 500 cars were garaged: outside about 700.

SOME DEFECTS REVEALED AT THE FIRST MEETING.

The new sport inaugurated on Saturday may, quite possibly, catch on. Of that I need express no opinion except to say that, personally, I was extremely interested in the racing, and that it made a better impression on me than I had anticipated. There were many defects in the management of affairs,

but here, again, the results were better than I had expected. Everything – so far as the spectators could see – went through according to the plans of a master mind, and the defects that obtruded themselves were obviously such as only actual experience could bring to light. These defects are capable of easy remedy in most cases, and I recognised in all I saw at Brooklands the existence of a determined guiding spirit that will at once remedy every defect as it becomes patent, so that anything I may say is not said in criticism, but rather with a view to assist. The first thing that strikes one is the inadequacy of the approach to Brooklands – and it is also the last thing to obtrude itself as one leaves. The road is so narrow and so many people seem to want to do so many different things, that from Weybridge station to the entrance takes a vehicle 10 or 15 minutes, the cul de sac at the end of the approach and the cross traffic adding enormously to the difficulty and delay. There is so much waste land around that the cutting of a second road from Weybridge station should be an easy matter. If getting in is difficult, getting away is worse, because everyone wishes to go at once. The charge for garaging one's car – 10s. – was generally considered excessive; whilst the arrangement was not at all convenient, nor was the accommodation suited to the charge. Visitors should be allowed to drive in with their cars and take up places from which to view the races, a fixed charge per car, including occupants being made, so as to get over the difficulty of checking the takings. The enclosures are satisfactory, taking, as one must do, the circumstances into consideration. But the dirty sand is a nuisance. There was scarcely a person present who was not covered with brown dust kicked up by people moving about the enclosure.

THE BEST VIEW OF THE RACING

is secured from the half-crown enclosure, and the way in which barriers to the 5s. and £1 enclosures are arranged prevents the people in the latter from getting a close view of the cars as they travel along the bank. Even with a pair of good binoculars it is exceedingly difficult to distinguish the numbers of the competing cars. The numbers are small, faintly painted and irregularly placed. The colours are seldom distinctive; whilst the practice of using two colours halved is most confusing, for one sees, we will say, a white jacket go by with a lead alongside the railway, but when the cars come into view on the other side of the track yellow is leading – to give place to white again a few seconds afterwards. The two clumps of trees on the left cut off a useful part of the track, so far as sightseeing goes, yet it would be a pity to cut away such a picturesque feature. However, when the autumn comes the gap between the clump and the hill might be widened and cleared with advantage. The bookmakers did not constitute themselves a nuisance, the noise being greatest in the half-crown enclosure. To those who desired to bet it was not disturbing, and even to those who did not, the bookmakers added interest to the scene. A careful study of the defects here pointed out and a few other points which affect the comfort of visitors will be well repaid, and I feel confident that the improvements will be instituted.

ONLOOKER. BROOKLANDS RACING — FROM THE GRAND STAND.

THE RACES VIEWED FROM THE PUBLIC POINT OF VIEW — EXPRESSIONS OF OPINION.

One's first impressions of Brooklands, as one leaves the railway station at Weybridge, is not attractive, for the moment one puts one's nose outside the doors, to be assailed – literally "assailed" – by a score of howling hooligans trying to sell sixpenny programmes for a shilling is not pleasant, and I wonder how many were

J. E. Hutton in his Mercedes racer at Brooklands, the car in which he won the first Montagu Cup and a prize of £1,400.

taken in. "Brooklands is only three minutes' walk from Weybridge station," said most of the papers in describing the situation, and so it is – but the track isn't, and there is not much change out of a quarter-of-an-hour by the time one gets in view of the racing. It is as well to remember this. Arrived there, the Brooklands Club, having adopted such an absurd and short-sighted attitude in regard to the Press, I elected to view the racing from the intermediate position of the grand stand, and so see

THINGS AS SEEN BY THE PUBLIC.

The first race was on when I arrived, and the first thing to attract notice, as I entered the enclosure, was the raucous voice of the betting man, a perfect chorus of "Four to one, bar two!" "Six to one bar three!" and suchlike shoutings, from a dozen brazen throats, making a pandemonium of sound in the narrow way. I read somewhere or other that there was to be no betting allowed. This was evidently wrong, for the betting men were everywhere, and at least served to enliven matters at times by their sallies, for they were, for the most part, quaintly sarcastic about the motors, and were evidently entirely at sea as regards the competitors, and their "offers" were very much shots in the dark in most cases. There were some "takers", but not a great many apparently. The heat over, I had time to look about me, and it must be admitted that the side of this hill, on a fine day such as we were favoured with, is a fine place for a lazy afternoon, and there is a beautiful expanse of country below, but although almost the whole of the course is visible from it, only little can be seen of the racing, or rather, I should say, it is extremely difficult to follow intelligently. Even with a good pair of glasses, it is next to impossible to identify the contestants – they are so far away – and as to knowing anything of what was going on, that is difficult, and much must be taken on trust. Almost the first words I heard when the first race was over and the betting men were quiet, fell from the lips of a man who had been down to the railings to see the finish. "Well!" quoth he to his companion, "of all the deadliest, slowest games I've stuck, I think this takes the bun!" and his friend did not dissent. The majority of those within the enclosure seemed to be motorists, but I heard little enthusiasm. The ladies mostly got excited just after the start of a race, when, for a mile or so,

HALF–A-DOZEN CARS WOULD TEAR ALONG IN A BUNCH.

"Oh! This is a lovely race!" exclaimed one gushing damsel behind me almost every time, but when one or two pulled away and the field tailed out, as it invariably did, her enthusiasm vanished. The starts were too far away for the men and machines to be identified on the line, so all glasses were directed on the cars as they came round into view from behind the trees, ere they disappeared round the banking to the rear, and here the spectators in the general 2s. 6d. enclosure had much the best of the situation, for they were able to see the men fly round the banking at close quarters and so got not only a better idea of speed, but were able to clearly identify the men, which we had great difficulty in doing.

"Who's this leading now?" enquired one man during the Gottlieb-Daimler Plate race, "Martin, isn't it?"

"What's his colours?"

"Can't see, he's tucked away behind the dashboard."

"Well, I think it's Martin, he's got a white cap."

"But – looking at the programme – there are three men with white caps," and so on went the conversation, and not one seemed really certain who was who till the telegraph went up. The race between Jarrott and Newton in the Byfleet Plate was, perhaps, the only one in which the interest was sustained throughout the race, and about which there was any real enthusiasm. Their

CLOSE RUNNING AND PASSING AND RE-PASSING

had attracted early attention to them, and Jarrott had been recognised by his white jacket and the Napier car by its shape, and when they made a dead-heat of it, the excitement was great.

"That was something like a race", was the general expression heard on all sides, and the crowd settled down on the qui vive for another – which didn't come.

Quite early in the day the entire supply of edibles in the refreshment tent was exhausted, and many were the complaints from famished people, who had had to go without lunch to get there in time, and had depended on finding food there; whilst another complaint, which was frequently heard before the end of the meeting, was from men who wanted to go into the general enclosure in order to get a closer view of the racing, but who found there were no "pass-out" tickets, and if they once left the grand stand enclosure they would have to pay another half-crown to get back in again! Of course, chief interest centred in the big race for the Montagu Cup, and many men expressed themselves disappointed that Nazzaro did not drive, whilst several said they had come expressly to see him, and the committee should not have announced him if he wasn't coming. *H.S.*

NUVOLARI: MAESTRO!
Nuvolari (Auto Union) Wins Donington Grand Prix in Brilliant Style After Losing Lead and Regaining It.
Dobson First British Driver

It is true to say that every Grand Prix in which the Formula cars take part is in its own way sensational. The very progress of these 400 h.p. 1-ton cars round the circuits of Europe is sensational enough. The Donington Grand Prix was no exception. First of all the speed, the noise and the very shape of the cars staggered the largest crowd which has ever watched a motor race in this country – over 60,000 of them, literally awe-struck during the first few laps and bubbling over with enthusiasm throughout the race.

Then sensation piled on sensation. Nuvolari leaped into the lead from the moment H.R.H. the Duke of Kent started the race – a signal honour for the Derby and District Club. The Italian led for 26 laps from Muller and Seaman at over 80 m.p.h. Then he stopped to change a plug and fell to fourth place. Next came the episode of oil on the course, which sent every German car flying off the road, put Hasse out of the race, and delayed Seaman a lap. Thus at 37 laps Muller led from Lang and Nuvolari. At 38 laps Lang stopped for fuel, without losing his place. Then Muller stopped and Lang led, Muller second, Nuvolari third. At 42 laps Nuvolari refilled but

RESULTS:Date: October 22. Circuit: Donington, 3.125 miles to the lap. Distance: 80 laps, 250 miles.

1, Tazio Nuvolari (Auto Union),	3 hrs. 6 mins. 22 secs.; 80.49 m.p.h.
2, Hermann Lang (Mercedes),	3 hrs. 8 mins.; 79.79 m.p.h.
3, Richard Seaman (Mercedes),	79.48 m.p.h.; one lap behind.
4, Hermann Muller (Auto Union),	79.01 m.p.h.; one lap behind leader.
5, Manfred von Brauchitsch (Mercedes);	one lap behind.
6, Arthur Dobson (E.R.A.);	six laps behind leader.
7, Billy Cotton–Wilkinson (E.R.A.);	six laps behind leader.
8, Ian Connell–Monkhouse (E.R.A.);	six laps behind leader.

Fastest Lap: Tazio Nuvolari's 63rd lap – 2 mins. 14.4 secs. Speed, 83.71 m.p.h. Receives Craner Trophy and £100.

Leader at Half-distance: Hermann Muller. Receives £50.

was still third. Nuvolari set about catching up, made up the gap of nearly a minute, did the race's fastest lap at over 83 m.p.h., caught Muller at 52 laps, caught Lang at 67 laps, and then ran right away to win by 1 min. 38 secs. at 80.49 m.p.h.

Kautz crashed twice on the third lap and retired; Villoresi (Maserati) and both Delahayes all retired. Hasse crashed and retired. Arthur Dobson led the British cars all through with some ease and finished only six laps late. Cudden-Fletcher ran off the course, Hanson and Maclure blew up.

The Race, by "Grande Vitesse"

Never has there been such a race in England. Never has such a crowd watched motor racing. A lovely autumnal morning, streams of traffic from every point of the compass, well over 60,000 people thronging to Donington. A signal honour for the race and its organizers, as well as for the foreign drivers; H.R.H. the Duke of Kent there to start the race. General Huhnlein, head of German motor sport and high in Nazi councils, came specially for the race, and with him the president and vice-president of the O.N.S. (German "R.A.C.") and members of the German Embassy from London. The grandstand packed, the military band playing, a crowd several deep right round the entire course, car parks black with cars;

there has never been anything like it in this country before.

Just before the start Dick Seaman drove the Duke of Kent round the circuit twice – one quite fast lap – in a fine 12-cylinder Lagonda, and Lionel Martin performed a like service for General Huhnlein in a Bentley.

Then the cars came in slow procession down the course with mechanics at the wheel, a sight which set the crowd buzzing with excitement. The line-up on the grid, engines silent now. The drivers get in, Nuvolari last of all in red helmet, yellow jumper and blue trousers. Seaman in a green helmet, Brauchitsch red, Lang white, Baumer blue.

Thirty seconds to go. The Duke raises the Union Jack. The portable electric starters whirr, the air shakes with the roaring song of the eight German cars, the British cars seem silent in that din. The crowd goes dumb.

Down goes the flag, the crashing exhausts howl to an ear-splitting shriek, and as one the field surges forward wheel-to-wheel.

As they shot for Red Gate, Nuvolari left the ruck as if catapulted. He led all round the first lap, Muller (Auto Union) on his tail, then Brauchitsch (Mercedes) – with his injured hand and feeling off form – then Seaman, Lang, Baumer, Hasse, Kautz, Dreyfus, Dobson (going marvellously) and Villoresi, after a sluggish get-away. And Nuvolari led the first lap by 3 secs.

Lap after lap the grand little Italian dropped the pursuit – 5 secs., 6 secs., 7 secs., 10 secs. – lapping at 82 m.p.h. On the third lap Kautz, who had been feeling ill for days, went off the road at Coppice, restarted and went off again at Melbourne, embedding his Auto Union in the earth bank.

On the fourth lap, while the crowd was still recovering, Seaman passed Brauchitsch into third place. Villoresi, 11th on the first lap, began to pass car after car on successive laps, ripping off the revs. with a fine crispness. Raph (Delahaye two-seater) came to the pit after three laps with the engine smoking, stopped again at eight laps and retired at 10 laps.

Muller, 14 secs. behind Nuvolari and with Seaman on his very tail, shot past Hanson (Alta) on the inside at McClean's corner. Dobson, 10th and easily leading the British race, was just behind Dreyfus (single-seater Delahaye) and holding him, but at 13 laps Nuvolari lapped Dobson, and at 16 laps lapped Dreyfus as well!

Maserati Gains and Retires

At 15 laps Villoresi was sixth, in front of Hasse and Baumer. At 16 laps he passed Brauchitsch, and at 18 laps a piston broke. Exit Maserati. Cuddon-Fletcher ran off the road at Melbourne and

retired. Percy Maclure (Riley) broke his back axle. The order in the British field was: Dobson, Connell, Cotton (E.R.A.s) and Hanson (two-seater Alta – which was slow).

At 20 laps, Nuvolari had pulled out to 21 secs. lead at 82.07 m.p.h. Muller (next up) was one second ahead of Dick Seaman, who was driving marvellously. Then came Lang, 4 secs. behind Seaman, Brauchitsch (half a minute behind), Hasse, Baumer, Dreyfus, Dobson and the rest.

Three laps later Dreyfus was out. Three more laps and the crowd roared – Nuvolari shot into the pit and had a plug changed, sitting calmly at the wheel. He lost 53 secs. and fell back to fourth place. So Muller led from Seaman (just behind him), Lang and Nuvolari. Seaman neatly slipped past Billy Cotton as they shot under the Stone Bridge. Wow!

Whenever he wanted to pass a slower car Nuvolari waved one hand to the flag marshals, they gave the signal, the other driver pulled over, and Nuvolari went by. The system worked like a charm – but imagine taking one hand off at over 90 m.p.h. down the bumpy hill to the Hairpin! I ask you!

Slump in Oil

Then, at 30 laps, Hanson broke a con-rod and dropped oil near the Old Paddock. The German cars flashed down the winding hill one after the other, and then everything began to happen at once. Cars flew off the road in all directions. They went broadside, they spun round, they went backwards.

Of course, My Man George (The Most Thrown-out Man in Europe) was on the spot when the Great Oil Crisis happened, and I can do no better than quote him, as I was seated in front of a lap chart and stop-watch at the time:–

"Hanson blew up completely, coming out of Holly Wood, and on the very fast downhill bend towards the Old Paddock dropped very large quantities of oil, likewise on the hairpin, and then pulled off the course near the Stone Bridge. Nuvolari, following him, sensed something wrong and in avoiding the biggest patch of oil got into a slide and went straight on onto the glass on the right of the road, recovered, went back on the road, and with a lot of dicing got up to the Hairpin and away.

"Brauchitsch was next. He got into a series of wild slides just off the road and back, spun round twice on the road, arrived sideways at the Hairpin and got round it all right.

"Next came Hasse. He went off to the right on the grass, then slammed across the road on to the grass on the left, took down some fencing, missed a hut and a tree by inches, slid on and finished astride the safety bank, thrown out of his car. Mrs. Craner (wife of the Clerk of the Course) was in the hut and got a close-up view. Hasse was unhurt and tried hard to impress on the officials that something should be done about the oil as he thought it a bit perilous.

"Seaman came next, travelling fast and apparently not seeing the yellow flag. Went out wide to the right, slammed across the road and ended up on soft ground on the left beyond Hasse's bent car. He shouted to the crowd not to touch the car and tried to manhandle it himself. An official said it was all right for officials to assist, and Dick shouted for them to push. Eventually they arrived and he restarted amidst great cheering."

After all this – which might have been a frightful catastrophe – Seaman was a lap behind and the order was: Muller (5 secs. lead), Lang, Nuvolari, Brauchitsch, Baumer, Seaman, Dobson, Connell, and Cotton's car now driven by Wilkinson.

At 38 laps (119 miles) Lang stopped to refill (no tyres) and was off in 33 secs. still second. At 40 laps (125 miles – mid-distance) leader Muller refilled and changed rear wheels in 40 secs., dropping to second place. At 42 laps Nuvolari made his second stop, refilled, changed all wheels and was off again in 35 secs. Is this pit work or is it?

Baumer and Seaman refilled on their 41st lap, a lap behind the leaders, Seaman in 44 secs. (fuel only), Baumer in

1 min. 19 secs. (fuel and plugs). Connell handed over to Monkhouse. Brauchitsch refilled on his 39th lap in 30 secs.

Sheer Wizardry

After all this Nuvolari was a long way behind, still third, with Lang leading Muller by 23 secs. Nuvolari rolled his sleeves up and, roaring with laughter, set about motor racing in earnest. He came through the bends with his elbows flashing up and down like pistons, the steering wheel jerking quickly from side to side – and yet all the time the car ran as if on rails, the front wheels always pointing dead on the line of travel. Maestro.

There's no doubt little Tazio was on top of his form. He is 49 years of age. He was driving a car, he said, last year was unmanageable. And yet he was driving as he drove 15 years ago, doing things no one else can do, and slowly catching up after his two pit stops to his rivals' one.

At 43 laps Baumer came in with the engine on fire and retired. Dobson, driving better than I have ever seen him, was 2½ mins. ahead of the next E.R.A. and sixth in the race. Magnificent. And then Nuvolari pulled out a fastest lap at 82.72 m.p.h., just to show them. At 50 laps he was 58 secs. behind leader Lang, 17 secs. behind Muller. At 53 laps he passed Muller. At 54 laps he was 39 secs. behind Lang.

Gradually the gap lessened. Lang could do nothing about it. I suspected his brakes weren't too good any more. Neubauer warned him every lap as he fled past the pits. But every lap Nuvolari drew closer and closer, still smiling all over his face, never making a mistake, changing down and braking at exactly the same spots on every corner every lap. At 56 laps he did 82.96 m.p.h. – fastest lap of the day. At 60 laps he was 21 secs. behind, Lang averaging 80.01 m.p.h. At 63 laps Nuvolari went faster still – 83.71 m.p.h., and closed to 12 secs. Lap by lap the lead vanished – 10 secs., 6 secs., 3 secs. – and at 67 laps the little Italian caught the Mercedes on Starkey Straight, pulled out, slammed his foot down, and shot past on maximum speed – about 160 m.p.h.

After that it was all over bar the very considerable shouting. Nuvolari ran clean away, Lang next, then Muller, then Seaman and Brauchitsch a lap behind. Seaman was actually about 8 secs. behind Nuvolari on the course, gained a yard here, lost it there, driving, in my view, better than any German on the circuit. At 69 laps he caught Muller and left him, running a minute behind Lang.

And so the last enthralling laps ran out with Nuvolari's lead mounting and mounting – 41 secs., 1 minute, 1:7, 1:15, 1:20, 1:30 – there was nothing Lang could do against this mighty display of sheer wizardry. And then, just after 3 p.m. (the race started at noon), Nuvolari finished amidst such an ovation as I have never heard in this country before.

During the closing stages Cotton took over again from Wilkinson, overtook the Connell–Monkhouse combine, and chased Dobson, but could never get near enough to hurt.

Nuvolari Mobbed

After the race the crowd mobbed Nuvolari, who was very affected. Never, he said, had he had a warmer reception. After the prize-giving in the stand the "Deutschland Uber Alles" for Germany and the "Giovinezza" for Nuvolari, his only thought was some food. He'd had only a cup of coffee and four sandwiches. He spoke little on his way back to his hotel, except to repeat how delighted he was at his ovation. "England is lucky for me," he said, "three times I have raced here, three times I have won." And Auto Unions, in face of strong Mercedes opposition, have twice won the Donington Grand Prix.

All honour to the little British cars, which went so well and reliably, only 20 miles behind at the end of 250 miles; and, what is more, winning the team prize outright, for both German teams lost a member en route.

What a race! And over 60,000 delighted spectators departed swearing to come back in greater numbers next year. Which reminds me, both Mercedes and Auto Unions intend to visit us again in 1939.

Starting Positions
Giving best practice lap in brackets

First Row (left to right facing up the course): Lang (Mercedes – 2 mins. 11 secs.), Nuvolari (Auto Union – 2:11.2), Brauchitsch (Mercedes – 2:11.4), Seaman (Mercedes – 2:12.2).
Second Row: Muller (Auto Union – 2:12.6), Baumer (Mercedes – 2:13.8). Hasse (Auto Union – 2:15.4).
Third Row: Kautz (Auto Union – 2:18.6), Villoresi (Maserati – 2:21), Dobson (E.R.A. – 2:24.6), Dreyfus (Delahaye – 2:25.4).
Fourth Row: Connell (E.R.A. – 2:27.2), Cotton (E.R.A. – 2:28.6), Cuddon-Fletcher (M.G. – 2:29.8).
Back Row: Maclure (Riley – 2:30.4), Hanson (Alta – 2:32.2), Raph (Delahaye – 2:36.4).

How the Order Changed
10 laps (31¼ miles)
1, Nuvolari, at 81.57 m.p.h.
2, Muller; 14.6 secs. behind.
3, Seaman; 15.8 secs. behind Nuvolari.
4. Lang; 22 secs. behind Nuvolari.
5, Brauchitsch; 30 secs. behind Nuvolari.

20 laps (62½ miles)
1, Nuvolari; leading at 82.07 m.p.h.
2, Muller; 21.8 secs. behind.

3, Seaman; 22.6 secs. behind Nuvolari.

4, Lang; 26.8 secs. behind Nuvolari.

5, Brauchitsch; 1 min. 6 secs. behind Nuvolari.

30 laps (93¾ miles)

1, Muller; leading at 80.10 m.p.h.

2, Seaman; 2.8 secs. behind.

3, Lang; 4 secs. behind Muller.

4, Nuvolari; 59.4 secs. behind Muller.

5, Brauchitsch; 1:32.8 behind Muller.

40 laps (125 miles – half-way)

1, Muller; leading at 80.07 m.p.h.

2, Lang; 48.4 secs. behind.

3, Nuvolari; 58 secs. behind Muller.

4, Baumer; 2:30.2 behind Muller.

5, Brauchitsch; 2:39.4 behind Muller.

6, Seaman; 7, Dobson; 8, Cotton; 9, Connell.

50 laps (156 miles)

1, Lang; leading at 78.77 m.p.h.

2, Muller; 40.6 secs. behind.

3, Nuvolari; 58 secs. behind Lang.

4, Brauchitsch; 1:58 behind Lang.

5, Seaman; 2:48.2 behind Lang.

60 laps (187¾ miles)

1, Lang; leading at 80.01 m.p.h.

2, Nuvolari; 21 secs. behind.

3, Muller; 1:4.2 behind Lang.

4, Brauchitsch; 1:59.8 behind Lang.

5, Seaman; 2:26.6 behind Lang.

70 laps (219 miles)

1, Nuvolari; leading at 80.29 m.p.h.

2, Lang; 17.4 secs. behind.

3, Seaman; 2:21.4 behind Nuvolari.

4, Muller; 2:30.2 behind Nuvolari.

5, Brauchitsch; 2:59.8 behind Nuvolari.

Other Awards

Team Prize: E.R.A. team of "independents" – Dobson, Connell and Cotton.

President's Trophy and £100 for first British car to finish: Arthur Dobson (E.R.A.); second (Derby Trophy and £75), W. E. Cotton and W. E. Wilkinson (E.R.A.); third (Leicester Trophy and £50), Ian Connell and P. R. Monkhouse (E.R.A.)

Pit Stops

Lap 3: Raph (Delahaye), oiling trouble. **Lap 8:** Raph again. **Lap 10:** Raph retires. **Lap 18:** Villoresi (Maserati) retires with broken piston; Cotton (E.R.A.) hands over to Wilkinson. **Lap 23:** Dreyfus (single-seater Delahaye) retires with broken oil pipe. **Lap 26:** Nuvolari changes one plug, falls from first to fourth place. **Lap 25:** Hanson (Alta) refills. **Lap 29:** Dobson (E.R.A.) refills in 1 min. 8 secs. **Lap 38:** Lang refills in 33 secs. – restarts still second. **Lap 39:** Brauchitsch refills in 30 secs.; Connell (E.R.A.) refills and hands over to Monkhouse. **Lap 40:** Muller (leader) refills, changes rear wheels in 40 secs.;

Tazio Nuvolari of Italy demonstrates his superb driving abilities in the Auto Union.

falls to second place. **Lap 41:** Baumer refills and changes plugs in 1 min. 19 secs.; Seaman refills in 44 secs. **Lap 42:** Nuvolari refills and changes four wheels in 35 secs. **Lap 43:** Baumer comes in with engine on fire; retires. **Lap 54:** Wilkinson refills, hands back to Cotton. **Lap 57:** Dobson fills again in 1 min. 1 sec. **Lap 64:** Muller stops to refix front "bonnet," 38 secs.

Fletcher (M.G.); at 17 laps (53 miles), ran off road. **Villoresi** (Maserati); at 18 laps (56 miles), broken piston. **Dreyfus** (Delahaye); at 23 laps (72 miles), broken oil pipe. **Hanson** (Alta); at 25 laps (78 miles), broken con-rod. **Hasse** (Auto Union); at 29 laps (90¾ miles), ran off road. **Baumer** (Mercedes); at 43 laps (134½ miles), on fire.

Retirements

Kautz (Auto Union); at two laps (6¼ miles), ran off road. **Raph** (Delahaye); at 10 laps (31¼ miles), no oil pressure. **Maclure** (Riley); at 12 laps (37½ miles), broken back axle. **Cuddon-**

The Grand Prix Filmed

If you didn't see the race, a film of it is being shown this week at the G.B. Movietone News Theatre in Shaftesbury Avenue, London, W.C., at approximately 10 minutes to each hour.

RACING DURING WARTIME

TRIPOLI WON AT 128 M.P.H. BY A 1½-LITRE ALFA-ROMEO
An Overwhelming Triumph in the Grand Prix – Record Lap at 132 m.p.h

Brockbank

The Results

1. **Guiseppe Farina (Alfa-Romeo)**, 393 kiloms in 1 hr. 54 mins. 16.49 secs. = 206.347 k.p.h. = 128.219 m.p.h.
2. **Clemente Biondetti (Alfa-Romeo)**, 1 hr. 54 mins. 45.96 secs. = 205.764 k.p.h. = 127.668 m.p.h.
3. **Carlo Felice Trossi (Alfa-Romeo)**, 1 hr. 55 mins. 9.36 secs. = 204.764 k.p.h. = 127.236 m.p.h.
4. Luigi Villoresi (Maserati), 1 hr. 55 mins. 23.56 secs. = 204.344 k.p.h. = 126.975 m.p.h.
5. Franco Cortese (Maserati), 2 hrs. 2 mins. 41.59 secs. = 192.186 k.p.h.

6. Carlo Pintacuda (Alfa-Romeo), 2 hrs. 2 mins. 52.33 secs.

Record lap, Farina (Alfa-Romeo), 3 mins. 40.91 secs., average speed 132.633 m.p.h.

The 1940 Tripoli race was blessed with ideal conditions, the normal high temperature being softened by an inshore breeze. Twenty-two cars went to the starting line, the positions determined by practice times being:–

    1. Farina (Alfa-Romeo), Biondetti (Alfa-Romeo), Villoresi (Maserati).

    2. Trossi (Alfa-Romeo), Pintacuda

(Alfa-Romeo).
3. Cortese (Maserati), Bianco (Maserati), Rocco (Maserati).

Behind these were five other lines with various Maserati cars. It will be seen that Nuvolari did not start, having decided as a result of practice times that his car was not fast enough to match the Alfas, and his place in consequence was taken by Cortese. Ernest Maserati was directing the official Maserati team and Constantini had charge of Alfa-Romeo.

Villoresi in Lead at First

The Marshal Balbo came to the front amidst applause and on dropping the starting flag the whole field got well away, except for Baruffi, whose Maserati remained on the line for 29 secs. Villoresi commanded an immediate lead followed by Farina, Cortese and Biondetti. This lead he held in a first-class standing lap of 4 mins. 2 secs., but in the second lap Farina unleashed his attack with a time of 3 mins. 44 secs. This took him to the front, a position confirmed by a third lap at an average speed of over 131 m.p.h. Villoresi hung on well, however, and the position at the end of the fifth lap was:–

Positions After Five Laps

1. Farina, 19 mins. 1.97 sec.
2. Villoresi, 10.56 secs behind.
3. Biondetti, 11.89 secs. behind.
4. Trossi, 15.26 secs. behind.

Shortly after this Villoresi came past the stands first, Farina evidently having had a spot of bother on the circuit, but this he was able to make up so that at the tenth lap the positions remained exactly as above. However, Villoresi was now only five seconds behind him and was, in turn, leading Biondetti by 5.6 secs. and Trossi by 10.56 secs. The position of the lone hand fighting against the team is, however, very difficult and there is little doubt it was only superb driving which was keeping the Maserati so well in the picture. Even so, by the thirteenth lap Biondetti was pressing hard at his heels, and on the following round managed to pass him, leaving Trossi fighting to gain third position. Thus, at half distance (fifteen laps) the positions were:–

Half-way Leaders

1. Farina, at an average speed of 129.4 m.p.h. (Alfa-Romeo).
2. Biondetti (Alfa-Romeo).
3. Villoresi (Maserati).
4. Trossi (Alfa-Romeo).

At the beginning of the sixteenth lap only 17 secs. separated Farina from Villoresi, but it was then necessary for everyone to refuel and here all the Alfas immediately gained greatly. In countless races we have seen the issue determined in the pits and certainly the time taken for replenishment had a powerful effect on the results in this

event. Farina was first in; his mechanics performed a marvellous job of work in filling the tanks in 24 secs.; no tyres were changed and he was indeed off like a flash. Villoresi, however, lost 57 secs., far more than he could afford, for Biondetti, who was then ahead of him, was refuelled in 27 secs., and Trossi, who had been just behind, in 36 secs. Villoresi was, therefore, now in fourth position and was never able to improve his placing thereafter.

Maserati Chances Disappear

Hence, from this point onwards it was obvious that the Maseratis had lost their best chance of winning, whereas Farina could go on confidently in the knowledge that he had the secure lead, derived from a combination of a fast machine, magnificent driving and pit organization.

The three Alfas were, by the twentieth lap, well established in the order – Farina, Biondetti and Trossi.

Villoresi was kept lagging behind, being nearly 1 min. after Trossi, and 1½ min. behind Farina. On the twenty-second lap Pintacuda (Alfa-Romeo) came to rest with a slight fault in the engine but fortunately was able to get going again and finished sixth. Meanwhile, Farina lapped steadily in the 3 mins. 45 secs., and proceeded to win the Fourteenth Tripoli Grand Prix at a speed which has only been exceeded on three occasions and in each case with an engine of four times the capacity.

Lang's last year's 1½-litre time was cut by 2 mins. 86 secs., but in congratulating the winner and the winning team one must not forget the magnificent show put up by Villoresi who, by acting as a pacemaker, contributed greatly to the high speed at which the race was run. Until the time when he had to refuel, the Maserati conductor had run consistently in second and third positions and had he not taken 21 secs.

longer than Trossi in refuelling he would certainly have occupied third place.

Follow Pit Instructions

It is worth mentioning, however, that the Alfa place men (and Pintacuda) drove in strict obedience to orders from their pit, and this good discipline undoubtedly aided them in securing the hat trick. Much credit must also be due to Constantini for his careful organization and accurate control, both of vital importance in racing.

So far as the cars themselves are concerned it would seem that the new Maserati engines were scarcely at their best and although they are undoubtedly the finest 4-cylinder engines yet built, it would seem that the straight-eight Alfa, with an additional 1,000 r.p.m., has an inherent advantage. Of the other runners it is worth mentioning that Taruffi took one of the older Maseratis into eighth place, and young Ascari, son of the famous Alfa driver who was killed at the wheel of one of their Grand Prix cars in 1924, took an old 6-cylinder type Maserati into ninth position.

No walkover. Despite a 1, 2, 3 victory the Alfa Romeo team had a hard fight in the Tripoli race. Twice Villoresi led in his Maserati, and only delay at the pits cost him third position. Below is an impression of his duel with Farina in the early stages in the first half of the race.

THE BRESCIA GRAND PRIX
Sensational Speeds in Italian Sports-Car Race. Sweeping Success for B.M.W. Alfa-Romeo Outclassed

The Brescia G.P. this year replaced the famous 1,000 Mile Miglia Race, and was nearly as strenuous for the unblown sports-cars up to 3-litres, for which it was organised. It will go down in history from many aspects. It was won by a German B.M.W. at a time when Germany is engaged in fighting a major war. It resulted in some truly astounding average speeds over what is a road circuit, despite its long straight-aways, one of which runs for as much as 18 miles. And it was a triumph of the open and closed sports-car. Incidentally, it proved that sports-racing cars can be very definitely impressive in action. The race was won by Hanstein and Baumer in an all-enclosed B.M.W. of 2-litres capacity. They set up a record lap at 108.18 m.p.h., and averaged 103.59 m.p.h. for the entire race. No tyre-change was needed, and Hanstein managed to drive for nine-tenths of the race. The B.M.W.s were controlled with typical German care of detail, and the standing lap was turned at over 101 m.p.h. The winning car had enclosed wheels and coupé top, and gave 130 b.h.p., or 65 b.h.p. per litre, at about 5,500 r.p.m. and Lurani and Cortese had an even faster Elektron B.M.W. coupé, capable of 134 m.p.h., but it ran

badly and retired after fuel feed and lubrication troubles on the eighth lap. This car weighed a mere 14.8 cwt. The winning B.M.W. was the last year's Le Mans car. The open B.M.W. weighed 11.8 cwt. It quite outclassed the new 2.5-litre six-cylinder Alfa-Romeos, Farina and Mambelli finishing second at 100.68 m.p.h. These cars developed 124 b.h.p., or 49 b.h.p. per litre, and suffered the additional disadvantage of 19.6 cwt., or some 5 cwt. more than the coupé B.M.W.s. Even so, road-holding was very good, and some schools of thought believe that Alfa would have won on a wet or windy day. Nevertheless, the best Alfa lap, by Trossi and Lucchi's saloon, at 102.43 m.p.h., does not equal the winning B.M.W.'s average for the entire race. The Alfas were put up from 4,600 to 5,000 r.p.m. in an effort to beat the German cars.

The other three 2-litre B.M.W.s were open cars with the modified engines and newly-faired bodies. All were lapping faster than any Alfa at the end of the race, until slowed, and all finished to get the Team Prize, Brudes and Roese being third at 100.0 m.p.h. Of the others in the big car category, the Lancia Astura and 2.8-litre Fiat were non-starters, and the Delage entries from the

English Watney stable were greatly hampered by difficulties arising from the international situation, Taruffi going out in the first lap with engine trouble. The other Delage held second place for a time, until it caught fire and retired. The weight per h.p. of these cars is about 16.6 lbs. per b.h.p. (135 b.h.p. at 5,000 r.p.m.) against 10.7 for the B.M.W. and 19.4 for the Alfa. Biondetti and Stefani (Alfa-Romeo) were fourth; Briem and Richter (B.M.W.) fifth; Wencher and Scholtz (B.M.W.) sixth; Pintacuda and Sanesi (Alfa-Romeo) seventh; and Trossi and Lucchi (Alfa-Romeo) eighth. Nine Alfas started. The race was over 922.7 miles. In the smaller classes some most interesting speeds were shown. Nineteen started in the 750 c.c. class, and Venturelli and Ceroni won on an o.h.v. streamlined Fiat "500" at 70.88 m.p.h. Cortese and Parravicini did the record lap at 74.64 m.p.h. Twenty-four Fiats started in the 1,100 c.c. class, and Fioruzzi and Sola's streamline saloon won at 82.47 m.p.h. from Bertani and Lasagni, lapping at 86.49 m.p.h. The new Ferrari "815s" were the fastest cars in the 1,500 c.c. class, Rangoni and Nardi setting the lap record at 90.77 m.p.h. before a roller bearing failed, while Ascari and Minozzi led from the start until a broken valve early retired them. The new Lancia Aprilias generally suffered tyre and minor engine trouble, but D. Ambrosio and Guerrini

won with one of these cars against a lone Fiat, at 78.47 m.p.h. Even if we add only 10 m.p.h. to the lap average as maximum speed, we have unblown sports-cars tuned to last 1,000 miles, achieving 85 m.p.h. in 570 c.c. form on 30 b.h.p.; 97 m.p.h. in 1,100 c.c. saloon form on 50 b.h.p., and 101 m.p.h. on 1,500 c.c. form on 65 b.h.p. – a real triumph of streamlining. It is easy to visualise marketable sports-cars of these capacities with maxima of 75, 87 and 91 m.p.h. respectively in unblown closed form, available to lucky enthusiasts who survive the war.

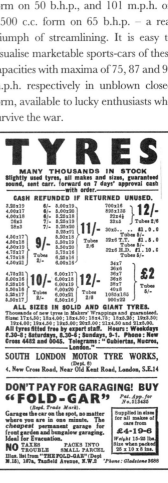

POST-WAR RACING

THE R.A.C. GRAND PRIX
First Event at Silverstone Dominated by Villoresi and Ascari – Gerard's Magnificent Drive Earns him Third Place – One Talbot out of Four Finishes

---

Final Result
October 2, Silverstone Circuit, near Towcester. 1 lap: 3.8 miles. Distance: 65 laps (250 miles approximately).

1. Luigi Villoresi (Maserati 4CLT/48), 3 hrs. 18 mins. 3 secs., 72.28 m.p.h.
2. Alberto Ascari (Maserati 4CLT/48), 3 hrs. 18 mins. 17 secs., 72.19 m.p.h.
3. F. R. Gerard (E.R.A. Type B/C), 3 hrs. 20 mins. 6 secs., 71.54 m.p.h.
4. Louis Rosier (4.5 Talbot-Lago), 3 hrs. 22 mins. 38.6 secs., 70.65 m.p.h.
5. B. Bira (Maserati 4CLT/48), 3 hrs. 18 mins. 53.6 secs., 1 lap behind.
6. John Bolster (E.R.A. Type B), 3 hrs. 18 mins. 57 secs., 2 laps behind.
7. David Hampshire (E.R.A. Type A), 3 hrs. 18 mins. 17.8 secs., 5 laps behind.
8. Roy Salvadori (Maserati 4C), 3 hrs. 20 mins. 10 secs., 5 laps behind.
9. Emanuel de Graffenried (Maserati 4CL), 3 hrs. 21 mins. 22.6 secs., 6 laps behind.
10. George Nixon (E.R.A. B-type), 3 hrs. 20 mins. 29 secs., 7 laps behind.
11. Peter Walker (E.R.A. B-type), covered 53 laps.
12. R. Ansell and G. Bainbridge (Maserati 4CL), covered 50 laps.

Fastest Lap of the Race
Villoresi's 4th lap in 2 mins. 50 secs. at 77.73 m.p.h.

Fastest Practice Lap
Ascari, 2 mins. 54.6 sec (75.45 m.p.h.).

A record crowd estimated at over 100,000 swarmed into the enclosures of Silverstone aerodrome for the first post-war Grand Prix of the R.A.C. last Saturday, October 2, under a sky which rapidly changed from grey to blue, and as the confines of the 3.8-mile circuit grew black with spectators, the sun beat down with almost summer warmth.

Neither the Alfa Romeo nor the Ferrari cars were able to compete, but we had two Italian visitors in Villoresi and Ascari who drive night and day to reach the circuit with their Type 4CLT/48 Maseratis, arriving just in time for four

Cars on the grid prepare for the start of the International Grand Prix at Silverstone.

laps of unofficial practice – in which Ascari made fastest lap of any competitor.

The two Italians took their back seat on the starting grid with great good humour, for their practice times were not eligible to count for starting positions.

The Starting Grid
1st Row
Chiron (4.5 Talbot-Lago 1948 – "two-cam" engine U/s), De Graffenried (Maserati Type 4CL), Etancelin (4.5 Talbot-Lago), F. R. Gerard (E.R.A. B/C type, Jamieson supercharger), Johnson (E.R.A. E-type Zoller).

2nd Row
Bira (Maserati Type 4CLT/48 – two-stage supercharging, new low-chassis tubular frame, coil-spring I.F.S.), Parnell (Maserati Type 4CLT/48), Walker (E.R.A. B-type), Rolt (3.4 Alfa Romeo – eight-cylinder, eight carburettors, U/s, self-change box).

3rd Row
Harrison (E.R.A. B/C type, Jamieson supercharger instead of original Zoller, C-type fuel tank), Comotti (4.5 Talbot-Lago), Rosier (4.5 Talbot-Lago), Bolster (E.R.A. B-type), Richardson (Riley chassis, E.R.A. engine, I.F.S.).

4th Row
G. Ansell (E.R.A. B-type), Watson (Alta 1939 with post-war body), Mays (E.R.A. D-type, I.F.S., Zoller supercharger), Hamilton (Maserati Type 6C).

5th Row

Hampshire (E.R.A. A-type modified), Nixon (E.R.A. B-type, Tecnauto I.F.S.), R. Ansell (Maserati Type 4CL, ex-Sommer with auxiliary fuel tank on body side), Salvadori (Maserati Type 4C circa 1934), Gilbey (Maserati Type 6C).

Last Row

Ascari and Villoresi (both on Maserati Type 4CLT/48 with improved braking).

The scene, as the cars did their warming-up lap in procession and came to rest, one by one, in their allotted starting order (decided, of course, by practice times), warmed the cockles of the enthusiast's heart. At least so far as the fast run through the pit area down to the bend at Woodcote beyond was concerned, the usually desolate appearance of an aerodrome had vanished and instead we had the true atmosphere of a Grand Prix. Two big stands faced the line of pits, gay with flags. Everywhere was black with people in holiday mood. In the enclosures the refreshment marquees bellied outwards with the press of persons within and over all was that odour of trampled, dewy grass which seems an inseparable motif of British outdoor meetings.

Music blared from "Mr Antone's" loud-speakers, now and then an engine would rev. up with a roar and die away again. The starting grid was a place of bustle, while officials marshalled the cars and mechanics put in the hard plugs. A unique feature, due to the width of the track, was the placing of cars five abreast in the front rank, backed by alternate ranks of four and five until, in the last row, the two lone Italians took their modest place side by side.

Up by the bridge Earl Howe stood with the Union Jack ready to start the race. Three times, at minute intervals, massed Lucas horns trumpeted the passing moments. Then, with a minute to go, one by one the cars started up until the whole field of 25 had burst into life and shook the air with the out-of-phase howl of exhausts while thin clouds of blue oil-smoke drifted up into the warm air.

Lord Howe raised his flag. It hung poised a moment and then, as it fell, the packed cars surged forward in that fantastic ear-splitting crash of sound which is the start of a Grand Prix.

As they shot past the pits de Graffenried was in front, with Chiron passing him as they went, then Bira and Gerard and Etancelin and Parnell and Johnson, all in a flurry of wheels and a flash of colour as they streamed past. Then, as they steadied for Woodcote corner, Johnson drew level with the leader, Chiron, and was about to pass and lead the race out of the curve, when there was a crash and a jerk; a universal joint broke, then the half-shaft flew free, and the E-type E.R.A. was out of the first race in which it has looked like showing what it really can do.

Johnson was lucky, for the flailing half-shaft tore a hole in the tank, then, spragging on the ground, shot up a trail of sparks which might have started a disastrous fire. Fortunately Johnson saw his danger, zig-zagged the car to free the axle and pulled up.

Salvadori (Maserati 4C) went straight to his pit from the start to change an oiled plug and was half a lap late in consequence.

Round the 3.8-mile circuit the massed thousands had their money's worth on that first lap alone. The speed, after the relatively slow 500 c.c. race which had constituted a "curtain raiser," seemed staggering, enhanced by the thunderous roar of the 20-odd engines.

Throughout the corners they swirled one after the other almost too fast for the eye to note the drivers. Tyres screeched, tails swung, bonnet missed tail by hair-raising margins. And out in front went Chiron's light-blue Talbot in the lead, Parnell's new Maserati on his tail, then Etancelin's Talbot, with Bira's blue and yellow new-style Maserati close behind and tearing through the field, Ascari and Villoresi.

That was the order as they streamed past after Lap 1 and then, as they whirled through Maggotts curve out on to the far side of the circuit, a flying stone hit Parnell in the face and the next instant another, ripping under the car, tore the fuel tank drain-plug clean out of its rivets and poured the fuel in cascades along the ground.

The Italians Lead

On that second lap Ascari and Villoresi were on Chiron's tail and on Lap 3 they passed him; then Villoresi shot past Ascari and so led the race. From then on, as was expected, the two Italians had it their own way and it seems likely that Ascari was content from the first to let his friend win or, what is even more probable, to wait until the last few laps and then, provided victory was safe, to have a real set-to together and let the best man win.

In those early stages the British cars, most of them at least a dozen years old and kept racing by Herculean labours of tuning, maintenance, replacement and repair, were outclassed, and even Gerard, whose car is always meticulously prepared and more reliable than most, contented himself with sitting back in eighth place – leader of the E.R.A.s – biding his time, for no one knew just how reliable the pair of Maseratis would prove. In past races they have sometimes failed, and Villoresi finished in second place at Turin on three cylinders. These two cars, I noticed, had somewhat different brakes from the similar models of

Parnell and Bira, with eight ribs per drum, and, I have a lurking idea, bigger superchargers as well.

Certainly, after the first third of the race Bira did not seem to have any brakes worth mentioning, and fell gradually back deeper and deeper into the ruck. Ascari, I think, used his brakes harder than Villoresi, which may account for Ascari's need of two rear wheels later on.

5 laps (19 miles)
Villoresi, 73.60 m.p.h.
Ascari, 0.4 secs. behind.
Chiron, 15.6 secs. behind Ascari.
Bira, 14 secs. behind Chiron.
Etancelin, 6 secs. behind Bira.
de Graffenried – Rosier – Gerard – Rolt – Harrison.

Comotti's Talbot likewise had brake trouble and after one stop he made another for good after only three laps. Rolt, too, went out early, at six laps, with engine trouble, and Watson's Alta, springing a leak in its tank, was finally parked on lap 8.

De Graffenried, too, was not having an easy drive, for his engine began to sound flat, its temperature sailed well above normal, and he was passed in successive laps by Rosier, Gerard and Harrison, so that at 10 laps we had:

PIROUETTE.–Hamilton (Maserati 6C.) having got into a little trouble at Stowe Corner, spun completely round at Seaman Corner and carried on.

10 laps (38 miles)
Ascari, 74.65 secs., leading by 0.4 secs.
Villoresi
Chiron, 49.6 secs. behind Villoresi.
Bira, 13 secs. behind Chiron.
Etancelin, 13 secs. behind Bira.
Rosier – Gerard – Harrison – de Graffenried – Hampshire.

Raymond Mays made an early stop with the D-type E.R.A. to change a plug – and someone overdid the routine top-up with fuel – stopped again a few laps later and after battling on in obvious difficulties he finally broke a piston and gave up.

There had been several exhibitions of undue zeal which thrilled the onlookers. Hamilton (Maserati 6C) knocked over three marker tubs on one corner, R. Ansell (Maserati 4CL) spun completely round on another, and Villoresi, too, overshot at Seaman Corner, ploughed the barrier, stopped and regained the course. Stowe Corner seemed particularly slippery through some

combination of surface and rubber dust from the screeching tyres. It is interesting that Gerard and Walker (E.R.A.s) were both reported to be faster than the fastest Maserati at Woodcote Corner.

The order of the leaders changed again at 12 laps, when Etancelin came into his pit, dropped right back, and after another 10 laps came in and stayed there. The car was boiling its water away almost as fast as it was put in. So at 13 laps, Gerard took the Frenchman's place and ran fifth, ahead of Rosier, driving very steadily.

Now it was seen that Chiron was by no means happy in his work. At 17 laps Bira passed him and thereafter Chiron clung grimly to his tail and Bira could not draw away.

20 laps (76 miles)
Ascari, 74.48 m.p.h., leading by 1 sec.
Villoresi.
Bira, 1 min, 29 secs. behind Villoresi.
Chiron, 4 secs. behind Bira.
Gerard, 35 secs. behind Chiron.
Rosier, Harrison, de Graffenried, Hampshire, Walker, Ansell G., Bolster, Etancelin, Salvadori, Ansell R., Mays, Nixon, Gilbey.

At this stage, Chiron was lapping in just under 3 mins., holding Bira, and Harrison was doing 3 mins. 4 and 3 mins 3.6 in pursuit of Rosier, Gerard was lapping a second or so faster.

The circuit was proving much slower than most had expected and there was a peculiar slipperiness about it that worried many of the drivers.

On the 22nd lap Geoffrey Ansell (E.R.A.) crashed at Maggotts Corner, the car rolling right over, but the driver, although shaken, appeared unhurt.

The order of the first 10 remained unchanged for the next 10 laps and then at 27 laps, while Ascari was leading by about four lengths, Villoresi dashed in for his first refuelling stop. The drill went like clockwork. The pressure hose was put in, in gushed the fuel, Villoresi took a drink of water, and he was off again to a push start in 40 secs. from first to last. Two laps later, which gave the pit staff just time to get set, Ascari came in. He, however, not only refuelled, but changed both rear wheels. The somewhat leisurely process occupied 1 min. 30 secs. from stop to restart, so that he now lay some 50 secs. behind Villoresi. Bira, slowing, was repassed by Chiron.

30 laps (114 miles)
Villoresi, 73.65 m.p.h., leading by 52 secs.
Ascari.
Chiron, 15 secs. behind Ascari.
Bira, 8 secs behind Chiron.
Gerard, 20 secs. behind Bira.
Rosier, Harrison, Hampshire, de Graffenried, Bolster.

The secondary struggle half-way back in the race between the E.R.A.s of

Hampshire, Bolster, Walker and Nixon was now beginning to resolve itself. Hampshire was having a tussle with the slowing de Graffenried, and Bolster passed Walker, whose brakes appeared to be failing, coming up now into the fringe of the leader-contingent.

Chiron came into his pit to complain that the rear of the Talbot was swaying and rolling and lost 45 secs., dropping from third place to sixth. Villoresi had added a couple of secs. to his lead, Bira (Chiron now sixth), lay 50 secs. behind Ascari and led Gerard by a few lengths until at lap 35 Bira refuelled and dropped 52 secs. Then Gerard refuelled smartly (with churns and funnel) in 48 secs. but Rosier, half a minute away, went past in third place. Both Hampshire and de Graffenried stopped, and Bolster went up into seventh place until he too refilled, at 39 laps.

Now de Graffenried was in and out of his pits about every five laps with his radiator boiling madly, but, at reduced speed, he kept going, driving to finish. Mays broke a piston, Gilbey retired and Chiron gave up (after another and particularly acrimonious argument with the pit personnel about rear suspension and tyre pressures) when his gearbox seized and oil flooded from under his Talbot.

40 laps (156 miles)
Villoresi, 73.49 m.p.h., leading by 49 secs.
Ascari.

Rosier, 2 mins. 6 secs. behind Ascari.
Gerard, 23 secs. behind Rosier.
Harrison, 26 secs. behind Gerard.
Bira, de Graffenried, Hampshire, Bolster.

At 41 laps Harrison's race was run, a valve broke, and Bira, slowed by lack of brakes, moved up into fifth place about half a minute behind Gerard, with Bolster firmly behind him, about 3 mins. away, and de Graffenried, Hampshire and Salvadori next up in that order.

The structure of the race was now set. Villoresi was a long way ahead thanks to Ascari's wheel change, Rosier ran third non-stop with Gerard closing up and bound to pass, Bira, slow but steady as ever, came next, then Bolster, and with de Graffenried always stopping for more water, Hampshire and Salvadori would probably pass him before the end. Ansell's Maserati, which had been at odds with straw bales and buckets here and there, was not going at all properly, and when he handed over to co-driver Bainbridge, the car was not fast enough to do any good and using gallons of oil.

50 laps (190 miles)
Villoresi, 73.45 m.p.h., leading by 42 secs.
Ascari.
Rosier, 38 secs. behind Ascari.
Gerard, 7 secs. behind Rosier.
Bira, 2 mins. 24 secs. behind Gerard.

Bolster, de Graffenried, Hampshire, Salvadori.

On the 50th lap Villoresi stopped for a mere 23 secs. for a final top up with fuel and, as before, Ascari did the same, in 39 secs., two laps later, so that he was still nearly a minute behind Villoresi. The former was slowing up now, and even Ascari was lifting his foot very early although trying to reduce the gap.

It was at this juncture that Villoresi could no longer read his revs. for the simple reason that the rev. counter shook bodily out of the board and lodged under the clutch pedal. Thereafter Villoresi had no clutch and had to pay more attention to his gear changing.

At 52 laps Gerard caught Rosier and passed him into third place – a magnificent show based on cool, steady driving with an engine he could trust – and began to draw away steadily but without closing at all on Ascari.

Bira was now nearly a lap behind the leaders and losing ground all the time, but Bolster, next up, was about a lap behind Bira and in no danger of catching him for fifth place.

60 laps (228 miles)

Villoresi, 72.56 m.p.h., leading by 30 secs.

Ascari.

Gerard, 1 min. 45 secs. behind Ascari.

Rosier, 6 secs. behind Gerard.

Bira, 3 mins. 39 secs. behind Rosier.

Bolster, Hampshire, Salvadori, de Graffenried, Nixon.

Now the race was virtually over. Villoresi was easing up, loitering around for Ascari to close in and make a nice one-two finish. Gerard, lapping at around 3 mins. and once in 2 mins. 58.2 secs., found it was not enough to catch Ascari and eased back to 3 mins. 5 and 3 mins. 6 secs. for the final stage of the race.

Both Hampshire's E.R.A. – now with Fotheringham Parker driving – and Salvadori were ahead of de Graffenried, who was pursued at a lap's distance by Nixon. Walker, also in trouble with brakes, could no longer corner at speed and, with piston trouble developing, dropped out of the picture, together with the Ansell-Bainbridge Maserati.

As the last few laps ran out the crowd pressed closer to the course and in the grandstand area, began to trickle and

MISSING HIS PEAK.–Etancelin, cap as usual back to front, frequently drove one-handed to shield his eyes from the sun.

infiltrate between the straw bales to see the finish. Ascari came up to 30 secs. behind Villoresi with five laps to go, and lopping off about 5 secs. per lap, narrowed the gap to 14 secs. on the last lap, but as Villoresi crossed the line at touring speed and slowed right down, there were a couple of other cars flagged before the second Maserati galloped over the line.

One by one the other cars were stopped and then the crowd, 1,000 strong, swarmed across the course and the drivers and cars at the pits went down under a sea of living flesh.

The race ran according to the book; for there was none to press the Italian Maseratis and the potential harriers – Johnson, Parnell and Bira – were all eliminated from that role. It was not the day for Talbot-Lagos, which finished one out of four and I doubt whether, even if Chiron had been running properly, his car had the speed to press the Maseratis or gain much from their fuel stops.

Grande Vitesse

Retirements

L. G. Johnson (E.R.A. E-type): Lap 1, broken rear universal and half shaft immediately after taking the lead at the first curve. **R. Parnell** (Maserati 4CLT/48): Lap 1, stone tore away the fuel tank drain plug and emptied the tank. **G. Comotti** (Talbot-Lago): Lap 3, defective brakes, while running sixth. **A. P. R. Rolt** (3.4 Alfa Romeo U/s):

Lap 6, engine trouble. **G. Watson** (Alta): Lap 8, split tank. **G. Richardson** (E.R.A.-Riley): Lap 12, transmission. **D. Hamilton** (Maserati 6C): Lap 17, oil pressure vanished. **G. Ansell** (E.R.A. B-type): Lap 22, crashed (unhurt). **P. Etancelin** (Talbot-Lago): Lap 22, engine. **R. Mays** (E.R.A. D-type): Lap 35, piston. **S. Gilbey** (Maserati 6C): Lap 36, gearbox. **L. Chiron** (Lago-Talbot): Lap 37, gearbox. Ran third during early stages of race, dropped to sixth after a pit stop to check tyre pressures. **T. C. Harrison** (E.R.A. B/C-type): Lap 41, broken valve when lying sixth.

* 25 started.

Some Fastest Laps

Villoresi: Fastest lap of the day – fourth lap in 2 mins. 50 secs. (77.73 m.p.h.).

Ascari: 2 mins. 52.8 secs. (76.12 m.p.h.)

Gerard: 2 mins. 58.2 secs. (73.9 m.p.h.) on lap 25.

Rosier: 2 mins. 59.3 secs. (73.52 m.p.h.) on lap 25.

Bira: 2 mins. 58.4 secs. (73.7 m.p.h.) on lap 7.

Bolster: 3 mins. 3 secs. (72.21 m.p.h.) on lap 27.

Chiron: 2 mins. 58.6 secs. (73.6 m.p.h.) on lap 28.

Harrison: 2 mins. 59.2 secs (73.51 m.p.h.) on lap 23.

THE "500" RACE

As the curtain raiser to the Grand Prix at 2 p.m., the R.A.C. staged the biggest event yet for the new category of 500 c.c. cars, unsupercharged, which has come into prominence in hill-climbs and sprints since the war, and which started at 12 noon, after Mr. John Cobb had completed his ceremonial (and heartily applauded) tour of honour to open the circuit in a new Healey Sportsmobile.

This being a 13-lap (50-mile) race, the usual half-pint sprint tanks were of no use, and ingenious were the schemes for fitting larger reservoirs on such scanty vehicles.

Fastest laps in practice had been made by Stirling Moss, that up-and-coming youngster of 18, in his Goodwood-winning Cooper, at nearly 67 m.p.h. (3 mins. 17.4 secs.), with "Spike" Rhiando next (3 mins. 27.4) in his glamorous golden-painted Cooper, and Coward third (Cowlan Norton) with 3 mins. 28 secs. The practice times produced the following field:–

1st Row
Moss (Cooper J.A.P.), Rhiando (Cooper J.A.P.), Coward (Cowlan Norton), Dryden (Cooper Norton), Strang (Strang Vincent-H.R.D.).

2nd Row
Cooper (Cooper J.A.P.), Brandon (Cooper J.A.P.), Coldham (Cooper J.A.P.), Sir F. Samuelson (Cooper J.A.P.).

3rd Row
Smith (C.F.S. J.A.P.), Aikens (Aikens Triumph), Saunders (Cooper J.A.P.), Grose (Grose), Page (Cooper J.A.P.).

4th Row
Stoop (Spink Rudge), Gibbs (M.A.C.), Phillips (Fairley Norton), Clark (A.S.A.).

5th Row
Flather (Marott Scott twin), Wharton (Wharton B.S.A. twin), Fry (Freikaiserwagen J.A.P.), Lord Strathcarron (Marwyn J.A.P.).

6th Row
Bosisto (Buzzie II), Smith (Smith J.A.P.), Underwood (Underwood), Messenger (Special).

The start was a trifle odd. As the flag dropped there was a sort of astonished pause, and then Moss and Strang alone got off the line, followed belatedly by Dryden (Cooper Norton), Aikens (Aikens) and the best part of the field very much one at a time. It looked as if the flag fell before the cars had all been properly marshalled on the starting grid. Moss was by way of being favourite for this race, for he is very fast and corners on the limit to gain seconds from possibly faster cars.

Strang, however, with the powerful Vincent H.R.D.-engined Strang, led Moss the first time round by a few lengths, but Moss passed on the next lap. On lap 3 Strang lew up on the course; the engine seized. Then, four laps later, while still leading by about 6 secs. from Rhiando, who had come streaking through the field after a bad start. Moss also retired with a loose chain sprocket. "Spike" then took the lead, lapping at well over 60 m.p.h. and half a minute ahead of John Cooper, constructor of the Cooper cars.

There was no catching Rhiando, although, half way through the race, he found himself being sprayed with fuel and sat, soaked to the skin; being in extreme discomfort, it is not surprising that he slowed down.

Coward (Cowlan), also after a slow start, came right through into third place

OVER-EAGER.–"Spike" Rhiando nearly came to grief in the early stages of the "500" race when, in an attempt to pass Moss on Seaman Corner, he got into a violent slide.

by half distance, but fell away at the end.

Cooper grimly closed in on Rhiando, but Rhiando was too far ahead and won by about 6 secs. clear. Coward dropped back with Coldham; Brandon came through into fourth place and then the race was over.

500 C.C. Race Final Result
1 lap: 3.8 miles. Distance: 13 laps (50 miles approximately)

1. "Spike" Rhiando (Cooper-J.A.P.), 47 mins. 10.6 secs., 60.68 m.p.h.
2. John Cooper (Cooper-J.A.P.), 47 mins. 16.8 secs., 60.55 m.p.h.
3. Sir Francis Samuelson (Cooper-J.A.P.), 47 mins. 47.4 secs., 59.9 m.p.h.
4. Eric Brandon (Cooper-J.A.P.), 47 mins. 48.2 secs., 59.87 m.p.h.
5. R. L. Coward (Cowlan-Norton), one lap behind, 60.03 m.p.h.
6. S. A. Coldham (Cooper-J.A.P.), two laps behind, 51.7 m.p.h.
7. R. W. Phillips (Fairley-Norton), two laps behind, 51.23 m.p.h.
8. J. R. Stoop (Spink Rudge), two laps behind, 50.24 m.p.h.

Fastest Lap

Rhiando, on lap 3, in 3 mins. 29 secs. (63.22 m.p.h.).

Fastest Practice Lap

Moss (Cooper), in 3 mins. 17.4 secs. (66.95 m.p.h.).

MOSS WINS MILLE MIGLIA AT 97.9 M.P.H.
Number Two in Mercedes-Benz Team Breaks Ferrari Threat and Exceeds Previous Best Speed by nearly 10 m.p.h.

History was made here today in the 22nd Mille Miglia run in unwonted summer sunshine. Moss won the 992-mile race with the 3-litre, 8-cylinder Mercedes-Benz 300 SLR at the record speed of 97.93 m.p.h., by nearly 32 minutes from his team-mate Fangio – sole survivors of four team cars – and despite a bump into straw bales which he had overlooked. He is but the second foreigner to win the race, the first British driver to do so, and scored the second win for the foreign car – Caracciola won with a Mercedes in 1931. Records went overboard in all classes, and Porsche underlined the German defeat of the Italian industry with victory in three classes at record speeds, and a win with the 300 SL Mercedes driven by the American, John Fitch, in the Grand Touring Class.

In the first few hundred miles, these amazing sports cars averaged 120 m.p.h. and the Ferraris showed themselves faster than the Mercedes, but more fragile. Moss led the Mercedes attack throughout. He took the lead at Ancona, lost it to Taruffi at Pescara, passed him into Rome and never looked back, building up an amazing lead without exceeding his approved r.p.m. – a

magnificent display of sheer virtuosity.

As usual, drivers came in tired and travel stained to report a litter of wrecked cars all round the course, but no fatal accident has been reported.

Spring and summer had merged this year to drench the flat Lombardy Plain in golden sunshine. Not since 1936 has the Mille Miglia been favoured with such glorious weather and, indeed, instead of apprehensive anxiety about slippery roads in the more usual rain, there was misgiving about tyre wear in the heat and the colossal speed now reached by the larger modern sports cars.

For 10 hours, starting at 9 p.m. last Saturday night, from the floodlit launching ramp in Brescia, the cars were streaming forth one by one on the long 992 miles around the northern half of Italy, led by the new class for diesel-engined machines. By the time the last of the unlimited sports cars started at 7.28 this morning on a day of brilliant sunshine with a light mist which promised heat to come, the small cars were already past Rome on their way to Siena, 683 miles away.

Brescia was in its usual turmoil of excitement centred chiefly in the glittering sliver 300 SLR Mercedes-Benz which started top favourite. These rather large cars are credited with some 280 b.h.p. for their 16½ cwt. dry weight. Fangio and King drove solo with Brescia-ized cockpits – i.e., virtually single-seaters – but Moss and Herrmann, preferring companionship, took passengers – Denis Jenkinson with Stirling and a works mechanic with Herrmann.

Farina, Villoresi, Ascari (1954 winner) and Behra were all absentees. The Ferrari counter-attack was led by Maglioli, Paolo Marzotto and Siginolfi, with the new 3,750 c.c. six-cylinder model and Castellotti, the new discovery who drove in the Lancia Grand Prix team, with the fabulous new six-cylinder 4.4-litre "Indianapolis" Ferrari stated to produce over 300 b.h.p. for a weight of 14½ cwt., and Piero Taruffi, last man to start, with a 3,750 model. Only one 3-litre, six-cylinder Maserati started, in the hands of Perdisa, and there was a solitary 3-litre, six-cylinder Gordini, driven by Gordoni.

In that same big-car class were the Austin-Healeys (Abecassis, Macklin, Flockhart and Donald Healey himself) all with open two-seater 100S models with disc brakes. Their main worry was that when the bigger machines all inevitably overtook them, the roads might be open, facing them with racing through normal Sunday traffic.

No official Lancias

The new 1,500-c.c., 135-b.h.p., four-cylinder Maseratis did not start, and Musso (third in his class last year) drove a two-litre "six". There were no works Lancias, John Fitch, the American driver, had one of the 300 SL Mercedes in the Grand Touring Class, where also were the Aston Martin DB2-4s driven by Wisdom and Frère. A third by Da Silva Ramon of Portugal, and the XK140 Jaguar hardtop driven by John Heath.

The only British machine entered with any real chance of success was Peter Collins' Aston Martin DB3S, a gallant but lonely intervention in what was really a battle between the industries of Germany and Italy.

Of the staggering entry of 648 cars, 533 came to the line. A breakdown of the classes in order of departure was as follows:–

Diesel Engine Cars, 10; Special Series Touring Class 750 c.c., 102; Normal Series Fiat and Lancia Appia, 84; 750 c.c. Sports, 39; Special Series Touring Cars 1,300 c.c., 58; Grand Touring Cars 1,100 c.c., 14; Grand Touring Cars 1,300 c.c., 34; Grand Touring Cars Over 1,300 c.c., 61; Special Series Touring Cars Over 1,300 c.c., 30; 1,100 c.c. Sports Cars, 20; 1,500 c.c. Sports Cars, 15; 2-litre Sports

Cars, 35; Unlimited Sports Cars, 30.

As expected in the unusual summery conditions, the pace was tremendous from the start. Fangio (Mercedes), third away in the unlimited sports class, overtook a 3-litre Ferrari in the first seven miles.

At Ravenna, 18 miles from the start, Bayol's D.B. flashed through just before midnight, leading the 750 c.c. sports cars at an astonishing 82 m.p.h., and, at Pescara, he had covered the 390 miles at about the same average.

Speeds down to Verona, 42 miles from Brescia, were remarkable in all classes. Cabianca (1200 Osca) averaged 108 m.p.h., Fangio (Mercedes) clocked 112 m.p.h., Kling (Mercedes) 112.8 m.p.h., Herrmann had an electrifying 119 m.p.h. In hot pursuit Castellotti (Ferrari) averaged 120.7 m.p.h., and Marzotto (Ferrari) raised this to a most incredible 122.7 m.p.h.

Fitch's Mercedes 300 SL saloon took a two-minute lead in its class at Verona averaging 104 m.p.h. in the unlimited Grand Touring Class, pursued by Casella and Gendebien on smaller machines, and then Da Silva Ramon on the DB2-4.

National Fervour

All Italy was in a ferment, listening to the radio and watching television, to say nothing of the million and a half who lined the route six deep, leaving just room for the cars to stream through. The Mercedes were not having it all their own way in these early stages, and the speed was nearly 10 miles per hour faster than last year.

At Ravenna, 188 miles, Castellotti led the race at 119 m.p.h., a Monza speed – by 1 min. 51 sec. Moss 2nd, Taruffi 3rd, Herrmann 4th, Kling 5th, Maglioli 6th, Perdisa (Maserati) 7th and Fangio 8th, his engine sounding off-tune. Paolo Marzotto threw a tread soon after Verona, damaged his shock absorbers and gave up.

At Ancona, on the Adriatic, where the road runs straight for long distances, Moss took the lead at 116 m.p.h. average by over half a minute, with Taruffi 2nd, Herrmann 3rd, 2 min. 21 sec. behind. Castellotti in the fourth place and Kling 5th, Maglioli 6th, and Fangio passed Perdisa into seventh place. Tenth place was being held all the way by Giardini's 2-litre Maserati with Masso on his tail in the 1500 sports car class.

Meanwhile, Bayol had passed Rome in his D.B. leading the 750 c.c. class at 77 m.p.h., and with two more D.B.s behind him.

Misfortune attended the Aston Martins, Peter Collins threw a tread on the DB3S, spun but recovered. He changed the wheel but in the next 100 miles the engine broke down. Paul Frère and Tommy Wisdom on DB2-4s both had clutch trouble and retired; Tommy on the end of a tow rope attached to a policeman's motorcycle.

Near Rimini, Flockhart (Austin-Healey) overtook his team-mate Lance Macklin on a section where a Lancia had ploughed into a dense crowd, and possibly momentarily upset by the sight took a bend onto a bridge too fast. The car spun and dived through the wall 20ft down into the river upside down. Macklin stopped and rushed back to help villagers extricate the sodden driver, but Flockhart was more startled than hurt. Macklin proceeded with the race, broke his throttle and finished on the ignition switch.

Now, indeed, the battle was joined on the dash to Rome, down the long straight coast road. Taruffi took the lead into Pescara by a bare 15 seconds from Moss, Herrmann 3rd, Kling 4th, Fangio 5th – all four Mercedes ganging up on the flying Ferrari. Castellotti finished with engine trouble when fourth, leaving Taruffi out on his own. Fangio's Mercedes was short of revs and in no good shape, probably due to trouble with the fuel injection. At Pescara the Mercedes team had a rapid stop to take on a little fuel to carry them to Rome without the load of full tanks in the Abruzzi mountains. And, at this stage, Taruffi saw his oil pressure flickering and foresaw the end of his efforts. The

Ferrari bolt was almost shot.

At Rome, where tanks were filled for the last time and rear wheel changed, Moss regained his lead and led Taruffi by 1 min. 49 sec. at 107.43 m.p.h. for the 542 miles (Taruffi's speed in 1954 was 98.6). Into the picture now came Abecassis and Macklin on Austin-Healeys, a remarkable performance.

GENERAL CATEGORY AT ROME

1. Moss (Mercedes), 5 hr. 3 min. 5 sec., 107.43 m.p.h.
2. Taruffi (Ferrari), 5 hr. 4 min. 54 sec.
3. Herrmann (Mercedes), 5 hr. 7 min. 6 sec.
4. Fangio (Mercedes), 5 hr. 14 min. 10 sec.
5. Perdisa (Maserati), 5 hr. 19 min. 1 sec.
6. Maglioli (Ferrari), 5 hr. 21 min. 50 sec.
7. Siginolfi (Ferrari), 5 hr. 33 min. 23 sec.
8. Giardini (2-litre Maserati), 5 hr. 35 min. 58 sec.
9. Musso (2-litre Maserati), 5 hr. 36 min. 41 sec.
10. Adiarnanzo (2-litre Ferrari), 5 hr. 52 min. 7 sec.

Fitch led the Unlimited Grand Touring Class at Pescara by 18 sec. at 101.5 m.p.h. from Gendebien from a smaller machine, but at Rome

Stirling Moss and Denis Jenkinson, in their Mercedes-Benz 300 SLR #722, on the Futa Pass during the 1955 Mille Miglia, in a shot taken at speed by Yves Debraine.

Gendebien led the class by 44 sec. at 93 m.p.h., Casella on the third 300 SL was 3ʳᵈ, Toscelli (V-8 Fiat) 4ᵗʰ, and Da Silva Ramon (DB2-4 Aston Martin) 5ᵗʰ.

Then more drama: A few kilos short of Rome, Kling running fourth touched a bank and the Mercedes crashed, the driver escaping with broken ribs.

Still piling up his lead, Moss tore through Siena and on into Florence with 6 min. 48 sec. in hand at 97.5 m.p.h. – almost 10 m.p.h. faster than last year's pace – with Herrmann second and Fangio third, all three Mercedes dominating the race in the closing stages. Taruffi saw his oil pressure vanish, and Ferrari's hopes disappeared with it. Steed (Triumph TR2) retired in Rome with engine trouble and Scott-Russell (Triumph TR2) had his dynamo break off. Brooke on the third Triumph TR2 kept going steadily. Fangio's machine was not motoring at all properly, and at Florence they had the bonnet open to small purpose. Fourth came Perdisa's 3-

litre Maserati, and the two 3750 Ferraris of Maglioli and Siginolfi too far down to matter. And now Abecassis brought his Austin-Healey into 7th place in the class, running like a train.

Up over the Futa pass, with its dizzy hairpins, the cars stormed into blazing sunshine of high afternoon, and here Mercedes lost Herrmann with a stone through his fuel tank. Without pushing his car, and now using his gears more often, Moss stretched his lead still further. Musso (2-litre Maserati) took the lead in the 2-litre class by 9 min. at 87.8 m.p.h., but Giardini, on a smaller model, repassed him into Bologna and then Musso retired, leaving Giardini to lead the class. Fitch led the big Grand Touring Class, among which John Heath's Jaguar XK140 was running beautifully.

Hereafter Moss took the Cremona-Mantua stage at tremendous speed which brought him into Brescia 10 hr. 7 min. 48 sec. after leaving it, at the record speed of 97.93 m.p.h. to win, amidst deafening applause, by nearly 32 minutes from Fangio. It was indeed a famous victory.

And, among the late comers who had a very creditable speed, Brooke brought in the little Triumph TR2 at an average of about 70 m.p.h.

PROVISIONAL RESULTS

General Category

1. Moss (Mercedes), 10 hr. 7 min. 48 sec., 97.93 m.p.h.
2. Fangio (Mercedes), 10 hr. 39 min. 33 sec.
3. Maglioli (Ferrari), 10 hr. 52 min. 47 sec.
4. Giardini (2-litre Maserati), 11 hr. 15 min. 32 sec., 88.06 m.p.h.
5. Fitch (Mercedes 300 SL), 11 hr. 29 min. 21 sec. 86.18 m.p.h.
6. Siginolfi (Ferrari), 11 hr. 33 min. 27 sec.
7. Gendebien (Mercedes 300 SL), 11 hr. 36 min.
8. Seidel (1500 Porsche), 12 hr. 8 min. 17 sec.
9. Bellucci (2-litre Maserati), 12 hr. 9 min. 10 sec.
10. Casella (Mercedes 300 SL), 12 hr. 11 min. 15 sec.
11. Abecassis (Austin-Healey 100S), 12 hr. 21 min. 43 sec.

648 cars were entered, 533 started, 61 were reported officially retired.

Classes
Sports Cars Over 2 litres

1. Stirling Moss (3-litre Mercedes), 10 hr. 7 min. 48 sec., 97.93 m.p.h.
2. Fangio (3-litre Mercedes), 10 hr. 39 min. 33 sec.

3. Maglioli (3.7 Ferrari), 10 hr. 52 min. 47 sec.

4. Siginolfi (3.7 Ferrari), 11 hr. 33 min. 27 sec.

5. Abecassis (Austin-Healey 100S), 12 hr. 21 min. 43 sec.

6. "Kammanuri" (3-litre Ferrari), 12 hr. 40 min. 42 sec.

7. Pinzero (3-litre Ferrari), 13 hr. 14 min. 1 sec.

8. Macklin (2.7 Austin-Healey 100S), 13 hr. 19 min. 25 sec.

2-litre Sports Cars

1. Giardini (Maserati), 11 hr. 15 min. 32 sec., 88.06 m.p.h.

2. Bellucci (Maserati), 12 hr. 9 min. 10 sec.

3. Stracci (Maserati), 12 hr. 24 min. 31 sec.

10. L. Brooke (Triumph TR2), 13 hr. 54 min. 52 sec.

1,500 c.c. Sports Cars

1. Seidel (Porsche), 12 hr. 8 min. 17 sec., 81.72 m.p.h.

2. Escollan (Osca), 12 hr. 29 min. 56 sec.

3. Lautenschlager (Porsche), 12 hr. 59 min. 52 sec.

1,100 Sports Cars

1. Bourilie (Osca), 13 hr. 1 min. 21 sec., 76.13 m.p.h.

2. Colantoni (Osca), 13 hr. 12 min. 27 sec.

3. Mobile (Osca), 13 hr. 18 min. 38 sec.

Grand Touring Cars Over 1,300 c.c.

1. John Fitch (Mercedes), 11 hr. 29 min. 21 sec., 86.18 m.p.h.

2. Gendebien (Mercedes), 11 hr. 36 min.

3. Casella (Mercedes), 12 hr. 11 min. 15 sec.

4. Bastellbato (Fiat), 12 hr. 24 min. 43 sec.

5. Da Silva Ramon (Aston Martin DB2-4), 12 hr. 43 min. 50 sec.

Special Series Touring Cars 1,300 c.c.

Mandrini (Fiat), 71.85 m.p.h.

Grand Touring Cars 1,100 c.c.

Viola (Fiat), 68.18 m.p.h.

Grand Touring Cars 1,300 c.c.

Frankenberg (Porsche), 76.44 m.p.h.

Special Series Touring Cars over 1,300 c.c.

Pescelli (Alfa Romeo Giullietta), 74.95 m.p.h.

Special Series Touring Cars 750 c.c.

Dalzier (Renault), 67.25 m.p.h.

Normal Series Touring Cars 1,100 c.c.

Morelli (Fiat), 69.61 m.p.h.

750 c.c. Sports Cars

Storez (D.B.), 74.27 m.p.h.

From 'Grande Vitesse'
Brescia, Italy, Sunday night, May 1

DRIVING A RACING CAR

'COMPETITION DRIVING', PAUL FRÈRE (1963)

I do not believe that any book, or any amount of training of the kind given in competition driving courses, will make a good driver of anyone who does not possess a fundamental, inborn aptitude. Above a certain level, driving becomes a sport, demanding of its adepts instant and accurate reflexes combined with perfect judgement. In this sphere, only those who enjoy an outstanding natural gift, and who take a profound interest in the subject, will ever reach the top.

For this reason, I had some hesitation before writing this book— I thought, for instance, of Stirling Moss, Mike Hawthorn, Tony Brooks or Jim Clark, who all started winning races in their very first season of serious racing, at an age when they could have had comparatively little driving experience at all. But surely, they are exceptions, and between the two extremes of the born champion and the hopeless incompetent, there must be hundreds of good drivers who, even if they cannot hope to emulate potential world champions, might gain immense satisfaction from taking part in all sorts of motoring events.

These are the non-professionals who, as a rule, cannot devote much time to their motoring activities and who will surely greatly benefit from all the experience that can be passed on to them, thereby reducing the time necessary for satisfying results to be achieved, in whatever sort of competition they intend to enter. If they have analytical minds, they will probably also like to have a better knowledge of the basic physics governing the behaviour and the attitude of their car on the road, which, in turn, will help them drive it to better purpose.

CONTROLS

Learn to be a good driver first! Who is a good driver and who is not is a matter for discussion. Obviously, your family would not like you to drive them to the holiday resort of their choice in the same way you would drive in a big rally or in a race. One day, while I was away racing somewhere in Europe, my wife and my children were driven home from friends living out in the provinces by a quiet gentleman using a big American car. Arriving home, the children said to their mother, 'How nice it is to be driven in such a smooth and quiet way; what a pity father doesn't drive as well as this gentleman!' But even if the sort of driving that is best suited to a Sunday outing is not exactly what is required of a racing driver, there are general rules that must be applied by both types—the observance of which, distinguish the better from the not-so-good driver.

CORNERING

In this section we will try to lay down the main principles of cornering, based on the natural forces acting upon a car when the direction of its movement is changed. The ability of a car to be steered derives from the adhesion of its tyres on the road. This adhesion is ruled by the coefficient of adhesion which varies with the state and the nature of the road surface and is directly related to the weight of the car. This relationship is given by the formula:

$$A = W \times E,$$

W being the car's weight and E the coefficient of adhesion.

Under good conditions, E lies at around 0.8. This means that if we want to push a car weighing 2,000 lbs sideways, a push of 1,600 lbs will be required. If all wheels are locked, the same push will be required to move the car forward or in any other horizontal direction. As long as a car rolls forward in a straight line, its adhesion, which enables it to resist lateral or sideways forces, remains intact. As soon as it is being braked or driven, or as it changes direction, inertia forces are created which use up part of the available adhesion.

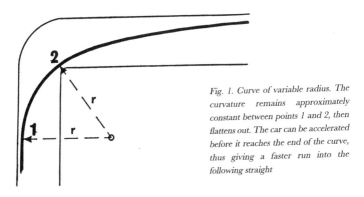

Fig. 1. Curve of variable radius. The curvature remains approximately constant between points 1 and 2, then flattens out. The car can be accelerated before it reaches the end of the curve, thus giving a faster run into the following straight

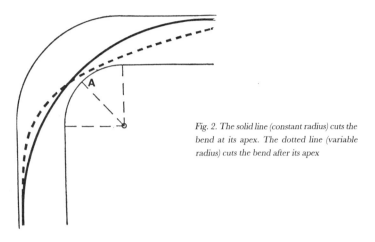

Fig. 2. The solid line (constant radius) cuts the bend at its apex. The dotted line (variable radius) cuts the bend after its apex

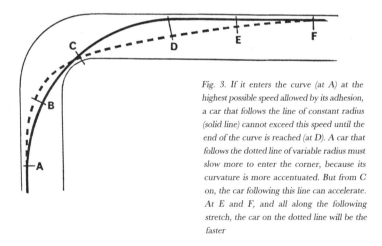

Fig. 3. If it enters the curve (at A) at the highest possible speed allowed by its adhesion, a car that follows the line of constant radius (solid line) cannot exceed this speed until the end of the curve is reached (at D). A car that follows the dotted line of variable radius must slow more to enter the corner, because its curvature is more accentuated. But from C on, the car following this line can accelerate. At E and F, and all along the following stretch, the car on the dotted line will be the faster

Let us first take the case of a car that has already been driven from a straight line into a bend, and which now rounds it following a constant radius and at a constant speed. In this condition, the car is submitted to a centrifugal force:

$$F_c = \frac{m \times v^2}{R},$$

m being the mass of the car, v its velocity and R the radius of the curve.

This force is directed along the line going from the centre of the curve to the centre of gravity of the car. It can be broken down into two components, one acting rearward along the centre line of the car, the other perpendicular to it and very nearly equal in force and direction to the centrifugal force itself as long as the curve is of comparatively large radius.

The centrifugal force being proportional to the mass of the car and thus to its weight

(the mass being $m = \frac{\text{weight}}{\text{gravity}}$), it is is also proportional to the vehicle's adhesion.

Thus the lighter the car, the smaller the centrifugal force, which shows that the often-expressed opinion that light cars are more dangerous than heavy ones, because they are more prone to slide, is entirely false. Of much greater interest are the two facts that the centrifugal force is proportional to the square of the speed and inversely proportional to the radius of the curve. The limit of adhesion at which the car will start to slide being reached when the main component of the centrifugal force (the one that acts at a right angle to the car's centre line) becomes equal to the vehicle's adhesion, we find that by making the fullest use of the width of the road to increase the radius of the curve along which the vehicle travels, the centrifugal force will be reduced for a given speed of the car. A greater safety margin is thus provided, and the speed can be increased further before the limit is reached. This is what is done in racing. The line of greatest radius that can be inscribed into a given curved section of road starts as close as possible to the verge of the road that lies on the outside of the corner, closes in towards the inside so as to put the car nearest the inside verge at the apex of the corner, then goes out again to the outside which is reached tangentially, when the car is straightened. In the case of a perfectly regular bend, the point where the car comes closest to the inside verge lies exactly half-way through the corner. This, theoretically, is the fastest way through a corner, not taking into account the phases of entering the corner and leaving it which will be discussed later.

The aim of a racing driver, however, is not to drive as quickly as possible round any given corner or bend, but to lap a given circuit as fast as possible. Surprising as it may sound, this means that the bends and corners included in the circuit will have to be taken slightly slower than the absolute maximum they allow. This is because every bend and corner must be considered in conjunction with the straight, or straighter portion of road, into which it leads. Every circuit is made up of bends, corners and faster stretches on which the car accelerates until it must be checked again for the next hazard. A straight is seldom long enough for the car to reach its absolute maximum speed; the progression of the racing car is thus mainly made up of bursts of acceleration followed by braking. If, to simplify the issue, we assume that the acceleration of a car along a straight is constant until the driver has to apply the brakes again, it is obvious that the faster the car comes into the straight, the faster will be its average speed along this straight up to the next braking point. For example, if one driver goes into the straight at 60 m.p.h., and accelerates to 120 m.p.h. before he must brake again, a better driver who has gone into the straight at 65 m.p.h., driving an identical car, will have reached 125 m.p.h. before he comes to the end of the straight. In the first instance, the average speed along the straight will have been 90 m.p.h., in the second 95 m.p.h. This is, in fact, not quite true in practice, as the rate of acceleration of a car decreases as its speed increases, but it shows that if the straight is long enough, the gain thus achieved may warrant a slightly slower average speed around the bend that precedes it, if this enables the driver to leave the bend at a higher speed and thus get a better run into the straight.

SLIDING

The slip angle reaches a maximum when the lateral force acting upon the wheel approaches the latter's adhesion on the ground. When the adhesion is exceeded, the slip is turned into a slide, when the tyre actually scrubs over the road. Obviously the angle of slide is added to the angle of slip.

Whereas slipping can only be provoked by a force acting in a perpendicular direction to the plane of the wheel, sliding can also be induced by forces acting in the same plane as the wheel, that is, by braking or driving forces.

The adhesion of the tyre on the road is the same in all directions. This means that if we want to pull a locked wheel in its own plane, we will have to exert the same force as is needed to move it sideways or in any other direction. Similarly, if torque

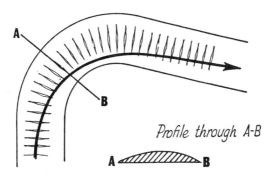

Fig. 4. Taking advantage of the road camber. If the road has a domed profile, resulting in an adverse camber on the outside of the bend, of which the adverse effect upon the adhesion of the vehicle is as marked as the correct camber is beneficial, the extreme outside of the bend must be avoided at all costs and the road must be treated as if it were narrower than it actually is. Moreover, the curve of the line taken through the bend must be adapted to the change of the banking angle, first being increased as the car gets nearer to the inner verge, then decreased as, beyond the apex of the bend, it is driven back towards the centre of the road

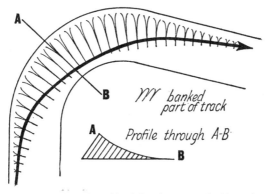

Fig. 5. The profile of a correctly engineered bend, featuring a steeper banking angle at the outside of the bend than on the inside, calls for an entirely different technique. In this case, the sharpest turns are taken at the beginning and at the end of the bend, when the car is nearest the outside verge where the banking angle is steepest, while the curve is straightened when the car reaches the inside of the bend, where the road is flattest

is applied to the wheel, the driving force acting upon the ground cannot exceed the adhesion of the wheel.

The important fact in this connection is that any amount of adhesion used up by a driving or braking force reduces the resistance with which the wheel can oppose a force acting perpendicularly to its plane. The constancy of the adhesion in all directions can be represented diagrammatically by a circle which has its centre at the contact point of the tyre with the road *(Fig. 6)*. The radius of this circle gives the measure of the force of adhesion. If a force greater than the radius of the circle is applied in any direction at the contact point of the tyre with the road, the tyre will slide; if the force applied is less than the radius of the circle, it will not move. All forces applied to the contact point (for the sake of simplicity we will consider that the contact patch between the tyre and the road surface is a point) can be broken down into (1) a force acting perpendicularly to the plane of the wheel and (2) a force acting in the plane of the latter. These two forces are interdependent; if a force less than the adhesion force is applied in the plane of the wheel (that is, a driving or a braking force) the resistance opposed by the tyre to a force acting perpendicularly to the plane of the wheel (that is, to a force that tends to make it slide sideways) will be reduced. Conversely, any force acting at a right angle to the wheel plane (that is, a force that tends to make the car slide) will reduce its driving or braking power. These forces are related by the formula:

Total Adhesion $= \sqrt{F_p^2 + F_l^2}$,

F_p being the force acting in the plane of the wheel and F_l the lateral force.

Thus, if a force F_p is put through the wheel to drive or brake the vehicle, a force F_l acting at right angles to the plane of the wheel $F_l = \sqrt{(\text{Total Adhesion})^2 - F_p^2}$ will suffice to make the wheel slide. Consequently, if the wheel is submitted to a sideways force F_l, the maximum driving force it will be able to transmit without spinning will be $F_l = \sqrt{(\text{Total Adhesion})^2 - F_l^2}$

This formula shows not only that any force applied in one of the planes reduces the ability of the wheel to resist forces in the plane acting at right angles to the force applied, but also that if one of the forces is equal to the adhesion of the tyre on the road, there will be no adhesion left to oppose any other force This means that if a wheel is spinning under an excessive driving torque or is locked in braking, it will not be able to resist skidding in any way; conversely, if the wheel is skidding, with no driving or braking force applied, it will not be able to transmit either of these if required. This explains why even an ordinary touring car that is being cornered steadily on a slippery road under a small throttle opening, will slide as soon as the

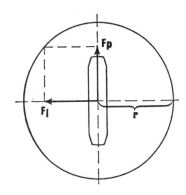

Fig. 6. r is the measure of the tyre's adhesion on the road. If a force F_l acts laterally upon the wheel, Fp remains available to propel the vehicle or, conversely, for braking. If a driving or braking force F_p is applied, any lateral force greater than F_l will produce a slide. F_l is thus the maximum 'total adhesion' available against sliding when a driving or braking force F_p is applied through the contact surface of the tyre with the road.
Total adhesion $= \sqrt{F_p^2 + F_l^2}$

throttle is opened wide enough in an intermediate gear to make the driving wheels spin. The power slide thus produced will stop only if the throttle is released enough to reduce the driving force to an amount compatible with the lateral force acting upon the wheel, or if the car is steered straight out of the corner so as to reduce the lateral force acting upon the wheel to a value compatible with the driving force applied. These are in fact the two means by which the driver can correct a skid.

Oversteer and Understeer

The exact point where, under the influence of an increasing lateral force acting upon a rolling wheel, the slide takes over from the slip, is very difficult to assess. The practical effect of either of them, however, is that the wheel rolls at an angle to its own plane. Consequently, they have a very similar bearing upon the attitude of the car, changing its direction of travel independently of the driver's action upon the steering. When, under a certain lateral force, the slip angle of the front wheels is smaller than the slip angle of the rear wheels, the vehicle is said to oversteer because it actually makes a tighter turn than the one corresponding to the geometrical position of the wheels *(Fig. 7)*. If the slip angle of the front wheels is greater than that of the rear wheels, the car understeers; it takes a wider turn than the one corresponding to the geometrical position of the wheels *(Fig. 8)*. Equal slip angles front and rear will result in a so-called neutral-steer car. In practice, a neutral-steer car, that is, a car rounding a bend with equal slip angles front and rear, will not exactly follow the line dictated by the geometrical position of its wheels, but will describe a circle of larger radius. It would follow the geometrically denned circle only if the slip angles were nil, or if the car over-steered very slightly.

The ratio of front to rear slip angle varies not only according to the car under consideration but even for one and the same car under differing conditions. Many cars behave differently according to the lateral force acting upon them and some are actually designed to do so. This is mostly achieved by using front and rear suspensions of different geometries, so that when the car leans to one side under the effect of a lateral force acting upon its centre of gravity, the camber and the orientation of the front and rear wheels follow different patterns.

But even if one wished to design a car possessing absolutely constant cornering characteristics, for example a car that would remain neutral whatever the lateral force acting upon it, it would be impossible to do so. The reason for this is that, under various circumstances, the forces acting at a right angle to the plane of the front and rear wheels respectively, do not always keep the same proportions. When it is being turned into a corner, a car will tend to understeer due to its own inertia; the quicker it is turned into it, the more will it do so. When the car is turned straight again, the inertia forces are reversed which will tend to make it oversteer.

This is hardly noticeable to the driver, however, as at the same time, the centrifugal force is being reduced, thus lessening the lateral thrust upon the tyres and reducing their slip angles.

For any given value of the centrifugal force, the component acting at a right angle to the rear wheels decreases more than the component acting upon the front wheels, as the radius of the corner decreases *(Fig. 10)*. Thus the sharper the corner, the less over-steer will be noticed and the more understeer will become apparent.

On a rear-wheel-drive car, the driving force is always exerted by the rear axle along the longitudinal axis of the vehicle. As the front wheels are turned, the driving force creates a lateral component upon the front wheels which becomes greater as the lock of the front wheels is increased *(Fig. 11)*. This obviously creates an additional degree of understeer which is added to the normal tendency of an understeering car, or can even momentarily induce a basically oversteering car to understeer.

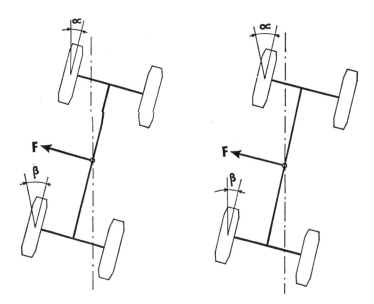

Fig. 7. Oversteering car a<b. The front slip angle is narrower than the rear slip angle. The vehicle tends to deviate farther from its original line of progress

Fig. 8. Under steering car a>b. The front slip angle is greater than the rear slip angle. The vehicle, deviated from its line, tends to turn back to its original direction of progress

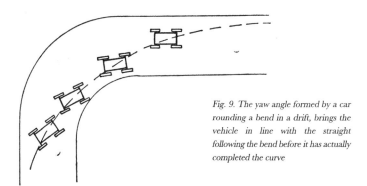

Fig. 9. The yaw angle formed by a car rounding a bend in a drift, brings the vehicle in line with the straight following the bend before it has actually completed the curve

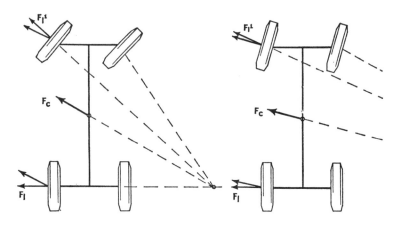

Fig. 10. As the radius of the turn decreases, the lateral component F_l of the centrifugal force F_c acting upon the rear wheels decreases more than the component F_l^1 acting upon the front wheels

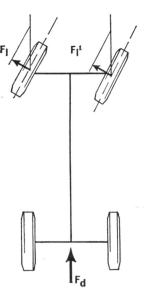

Fig. 11. In a rear-wheel-drive car, the driving force F_d creates a lateral component force (F_1 and F_1^1) acting upon the front wheels as these are turned into a curve

OVERTAKING

One of the main problems which arise from having a number of cars racing on the same circuit is that, on bends and corners, one single car uses up the entire width of the road. This means that when two cars are racing side by side along a straight, one must give way to the other when they come up to the next corner. The rule normally applicable in motor racing – that one should drive on the right and pass on the left—does not strictly apply to corners, where it is common practice to pass where it is safer or easier to do so. The question arises therefore which of two cars racing neck and neck towards a corner has right of way over the other? The answer is: the one who gets there first or the one who is best placed to nip into the corner first. Of the two drivers, one may have slightly stronger nerves and leave his braking until a few yards later, which will give him the advantage and enable him to get in front; if braking does not bring about a decision, then the driver who holds the inside position has the obvious advantage of being able to take a shorter course and therefore the corner is his. At any time *before* a driver has set his car on a given line for a corner, other drivers may try and get an advantage over him; but once a car is set on its line, it is *not* permissible to cut across it and force the other driver to alter his course, which could have disastrous results.

But where then, it will be asked, can a better driver pass a slower competitor driving a car of equal performance, if this cannot be done on corners where the better driver can use his ability to the best advantage? One answer has already been given: in the braking area preceding a corner. If one driver goes round the corner slower than the other, he must of necessity brake earlier and this will give the better driver a chance to pass him in the braking area. However, this is feasible only before slow corners where the braking area is long enough for the passing to be performed. In other cases, the better driver who has been unable to pass before the corner will be baulked by the slower driver and will have to take the corner at the same slower speed. Assuming both cars to have equal performance, the driver behind will not be able to pass his rival before the next corner, where the same story will repeat itself and cost the better driver a lot of valuable time. Unless the circuit includes a straight long enough to offer an opportunity of passing by taking advantage of the slipstream of the car in front, the only chance of passing a slower driver whose car matches the performance of your own, is to slow down and let him take a lead corresponding to what you think you can gain on him in the next corner. This will prevent you from being baulked and, having taken the bend faster, you will leave it faster and easily pass the other car before it has picked up enough speed to match yours.

The third method of passing is—as has been hinted at before—slipstreaming. An area of reduced air pressure is produced behind any car that is being driven at high speed; this reduced pressure will lessen the air drag of a car that is being driven close behind, thus increasing its speed. Slower cars can take advantage of this to 'get a tow' from faster cars, and in the case of two cars of identical maximum speed following each other, the second one will quickly close up on the first, thanks to the reduced air resistance. If its driver pulls out at the last possible moment, he will be able to pass the first car before air drag reduces his speed to its normal maximum.

LESS BRAKING—MORE SPEED

If you want to go fast, keep off the brakes! I will never forget a scene I witnessed at Spa during practice for the Belgian Grand Prix of 1953. The Maserati factory had entered four cars—three for the regular team of Fangio, Gonzalez and Bonetto, and a fourth car for the former Belgian champion, the late Johnny Claes. Try as he might, Claes could not nearly match the times of Fangio and Gonzalez. After much fruitless hard trying, Claes, who was a close friend of Fangio's, approached him and asked him if he would try his car because he thought it was slower than the others. Fangio immediately agreed; he jumped into Claes's car and did three or four laps, the fastest of which was just about as fast as he had done in his own car. When Fangio came back into the pits, Claes shrugged his shoulders and said, 'But tell me, how on earth do you do it?' Fangio said nothing at first and extricated himself from the cockpit; he then went quietly to sit on the pit counter, with Claes following him and, in his broken English, gave his very plain and simple explanation: 'Less brakes,' he said, 'and more accelerator.'

The assertion that speed is increased as less use is made of the brakes is, of course, a fallacy. To go fast, the brakes must be used, and used very hard indeed, but only where it is essential to slow the car down. For obvious reasons, much more unnecessary use is made of the brakes on the road than on a circuit which the driver knows perfectly. On the road any driver has a strong instinctive tendency to use his brakes as soon as he is not absolutely sure of what lies ahead. More concentration and better observation of any signs which may give a clue as to what is coming up, will help reduce the number of unnecessary applications of the brakes and enable the speed to be maintained at a higher average. To achieve high road averages, it is essential first of all to concentrate on avoiding unnecessary braking and it certainly takes a lot of concentration before this becomes a natural habit. But while it saves time, it also helps to save tyres, brakes and fuel. It can confidently be said that the merit of a driver is inversely proportional to the number of times he applies his brakes unnecessarily for a given mileage.

Some corners may involve a problem for a driver new to them. Not all are ideally shaped or regularly banked. Some may have an irregular contour, a decreasing or an increasing radius, or, in fact, be made up of a succession of two or more bends in the same direction, which are best taken in one single sweep. In such cases, the correct line through the corner does not necessarily bring the car nearest to the inside verge more or less half-way through the bend, and the correct point to aim at is not always easy to find. Figures 12, 13 and 14 show three examples of such curves.

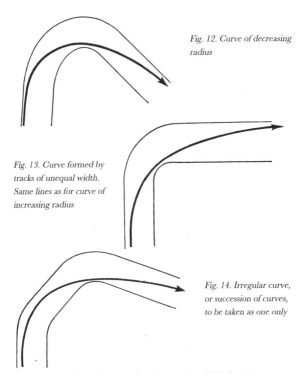

Fig. 12. Curve of decreasing radius

Fig. 13. Curve formed by tracks of unequal width. Same lines as for curve of increasing radius

Fig. 14. Irregular curve, or succession of curves, to be taken as one only

TWO HOURS TO GO

It's race day. Even for the most experienced racing driver, it is almost impossible not to feel a bit nervous when an important race lies ahead. If he did not, he could only be accused of lack of interest or lack of imagination. Though the reasons for this nervousness are difficult to analyse, it seems certain that fear caused by the risk involved in every high-speed motoring competition must play an important part. As far as I am concerned, I have always found myself much more nervous before a race in which I stood a good chance of success, than where it was obvious from the start that I would be unable to graduate out of the ranks of the also-rans. This is quite understandable, because when victory seems to be within reach, one is usually prepared to take more risks to secure it, not to mention the greater disappointment that failure will cause. But I have also found that somehow my nervousness could be traced to the fear of making a mess of the start. I always used to be much more nervous before a short race, where a good start is vitally important, than before a long one: for some reason Le Mans starts have always been much kinder on my nerves than massed starts with the engine running, and even very important long distance races made me hardly nervous at all if it had been decided that the burden of starting would be carried by my co-driver.

The biggest trouble is that when you are a member of a well-organised team, there is absolutely nothing you can do to distract your attention from the race before it starts. Your main pre-occupation then is to try and find out if it is going to rain or be fine, whether it is going to be cold or very hot, what sort of tyres—fine-weather or rain tyres—to use, or what your race tactics should be.

Choice of Race Wear

These are not idle thoughts though, and the question of race wear is a particularly important one. The cockpit of a racing car is always a very hot place—even when the car is a rear-engined one a lot of heat is carried into the cockpit from the front radiator and radiated by the pipes running through the cockpit. The only exception among modern racing cars is the Porsche which has a rear-mounted air-cooled engine. Even where the cockpit is open, modern wrap-round windscreens are so efficient that the draught cannot be relied upon to carry the heat away. This, and the fact that after some time the driver warms up to his job, means that after considering the prevalent weather conditions, one's choice of dress for the race usually turns out to be too warm. So the rule should be always to dress as lightly as can reasonably be thought possible. In most cases when the weather is fine, light cotton trousers and a light, short-sleeved shirt will be the most comfortable race wear. It is certainly a good safety measure to have these impregnated for fireproofing and some drivers even rule out short sleeves on the grounds that they give insufficient protection against fire. Nylon is particularly dangerous in case of fire and should never be used for any racing wear or underwear; even the socks should be wool or cotton. On the same grounds, and also because of the increased danger of burns in case the pipe leading to the oil-pressure gauge should break, shorts cannot be recommended, tempting as they may be, except for saloon-car racing where this danger hardly exists. Another safety measure against fire is to rule out one-piece overalls because in a case of emergency, these are much harder to remove than two-piece gear.

Tyre companies such as Dunlop, Avon and Pirelli produce perfectly waterproof two-piece rubber overalls. They should not be worn directly over the bare skin however, as water will always manage to seep in, if only around the neck, and will create a most unwelcome sensation of humidity and cold. Being more or less airtight as well as waterproof, these overalls are extremely hot when it is not raining and my personal opinion is that unless it is almost certain to be raining during the race, it is preferable not to wear them and take a chance on being drenched. Unless it rains very hard, the wrap-round windscreen of a modern single-seater racing car is so efficient that the driver hardly gets wet at all, though it may be useful to wear the rubber trousers, for protection against the water that splashes up through the joints of the body floor.

If the weather is uncertain, the question of whether to use goggles or a visor will also arise. In fine weather, I strongly favour goggles because they cause less distortion, and any dirt that may deposit itself on the lenses, being nearer the eyes than on a visor, is more out of focus and less disturbing. During most of my racing career, I have used rubber-framed flexible goggles, mainly because they are unbreakable and afford an excellent wide field of vision. They are certainly more liable to scratching than goggles made of unbreakable glass, but being cheap they can be replaced frequently.

In rain, all goggles will mist up unless they have previously been treated with some anti-mist compound that is applied to the inside of the lenses. But even then, they will not resist more than about fifteen minutes of rain. If no anti-mist compound is available, a trace of soap applied to the inside of the dry lenses and rubbed clear with a rag will do the trick just as well as most anti-mist compounds.

If heavy rain is anticipated, a visor will have to be used, and even this should be treated against misting. Some drivers favour a visor even in fine weather because goggles can give rise to perspiration and even irritation around the frame. But the wind will usually cause the visor to vibrate slightly and thus blur the vision, spoiling its accuracy, and in a front-engined car it is also likely to catch the fumes, sometimes to the extent of incommoding the driver.

If extremely hot weather rather than rain is to be expected during the race, measures should be taken to introduce air into the cockpit wherever possible. Slots and openings should be cut in the body, but only a short time before the race: if they are cut earlier, it can almost be guaranteed that the race will be run in a thunderstorm. Some drivers have used the simple expedient of removing complete body panels where this was practicable, to introduce more air into the cockpit; on a fast circuit, however, this may affect the maximum speed of the car, due to the adverse effect upon the streamlining. Cutting down the sides of the wrap-round windscreen to increase the draught has much the same effect.

Gloves must always be worn, as they not only improve the grip on the steering wheel, but also prevent the formation of blisters, especially on the hand that operates the gear change. Even if the change appears to be quite smooth, the skin of the hand will hardly resist the strain of the 1,500 to 5,000 operations of the gear lever that are necessary in 'around the houses' races like the Monte Carlo or the Pau Grands Prix, or in a long-distance event like the Le Mans 24 hours race or the Nürburgring 1,000 kilometre race.

In hot weather, the best gloves are those of which the back part is well aerated by large holes or wide-mesh webbing, while chamois leather gloves are very useful in rain, as they facilitate wiping water off the goggles or the visor. Alternatively, a piece of chamois leather may be sewn on the back of the glove, and it is always a good precaution to have a bigger chamois leather handy in a small box where it can be reached easily and where it is sheltered from oil, dust and grit. But make sure that this leather is firmly secured to the car by a piece of string, otherwise, the wind is quite likely to blow it away at the first chance.

Choice of Tyres

Another decision that will have to be taken which depends on the weather is whether to use normal or rain tyres. Rain tyres have a higher rate of wear, usually a slightly greater rolling resistance and may slightly upset the handling of the car if they are used on dry roads. They should therefore be tried in practice in the dry for a few laps, on a circuit on which they might be used, to enable the driver better to appreciate the pros and cons, in case the weather conditions turn out better than expected during the race.

If you are a member of an organised team, this will probably be the last decision you will have to take before the start of the race. However, if you have a reliable and enthusiastic friend who knows something about motor racing and who can use a stop watch properly, he may be quite useful for some private signalling. If you do not happen to be the star of the team, team managers are apt to neglect you somewhat and signal you rather casually and at long intervals. They may also deliberately give false information, for instance signal a very good lap time, say three or four seconds faster than you are actually doing because for some reason they want you to go even slower; or they may signal a rather indifferent time, making signs to go faster, if they want you to go quicker while you are already doing your best. I have always preferred to know the truth and to be precisely informed of what is happening behind me and in front of me, in order to be my own judge of what to do—even within the frame of team orders— instead of being instructed to go faster or slower without knowing the exact reason why. This friend should settle down somewhere far away from the pits (because team managers usually do not like this sort of private signalling) and at a point where the cars come out of a slow corner so that there is plenty of time for the driver to see the signals. Another wise precaution is to give him a note stating your blood group and rhesus and make sure that he puts it into his briefcase, so he has it handy in case you have a bad accident. This is information which the team manager should also have and, as a further precaution, you may also write it down on your competition licence.

The pre-race interval may well be used for quickly going through the main points of the rules again. All races are of course run according to the same general pattern laid down by the F.I.A. for each particular kind of event. In most cases, however, there are a few 'local' rules which should be known by the driver and the pit staff. For instance: is it permissible to push start the car after a pit stop? Is one allowed to call upon the help of marshals to put the car back on to the road or to restart a stalled engine if one has made a mistake out on the course? May one stop at the pits and restart without stopping the engine? How many people are allowed to work on the car while it is stopped at the pits? In some races, especially long-distance races such as the Le Mans 24 hours race, the rules are so complicated that they must be studied very carefully and a long time in advance; they should be thoroughly understood by the driver as well as by the pit personnel, as any mistake may bring about immediate disqualification.

TIME-KEEPING AND SIGNALS

The time-keeper must have at least two stop watches—one with two fingers, one of which may be stopped at will—or three stop watches with one finger only. Two of these, or the one with two fingers, will be used to time every single lap completed by the car. The other stop watch is used to measure the gap between your car and the cars directly in front or behind. A further stop watch, or another with two fingers, will enable him to get both answers on the same lap *(Fig. 15)*.

These intervals may seem much more important than the actual lap times, but this is hardly so. Knowing the times which have been achieved during practice, the lap times put up by the car in the race will enable the pit staff to judge if the driver is really trying, or if he may be expected to go appreciably faster yet. The elapsed time will also show when the car may be expected in the pit area, so that any signals necessary can be shown at the correct moment. This is particularly important during the night hours of a long-distance race, when it is extremely difficult to identify the cars as they approach.

Signalling should be done with figures and letters which are as large as possible, especially when the pit area is situated at a point where the cars reach a very high speed. It is quite a problem for a driver speeding past the pits at perhaps 130 or 140 m.p.h. readily to identify his signal, which should therefore be made as recognisable as possible or be given by a person wearing clothing of a bright and easily identifiable colour. It is absolutely essential that the signals are given at a point where the driver can devote his attention to them without danger. They must never be given in a zone in which the driver must pick his line for a bend that lies ahead or in a braking area. I once crashed a car in

Fig. 15. Two-finger chronograph; one finger shows the elapsed time; the other can be stopped at any given moment and catches the main finger as soon as it is released. The exact time of passage of several cars can be noted in quick succession and their lap times calculated

practice before a race, because on their own initiative, my pit attendants had elected to give me signals from the pit nearest to their van, which lay just about where I had to start setting the car for the following bend; my attention was retained a little too long by the sign—which brought me off my line—and I could not avoid crashing. Where the pit is badly situated for signalling, you should try to arrange to have another signalling post in a more convenient place. The best spot is the exit from a hairpin bend, before the cars have had time to regain speed.

If he is to go really fast, a racing driver must entirely concentrate on his driving. Therefore the signals must be as simple and readily understandable as possible. For instance, a driver is not interested in the number of laps he has already completed in the race; what he wants to know is the number of laps to go. So if he is driving in a 50-lap race and has just completed for instance his 38th lap, the sign to be shown is not L38, which would force him to calculate himself that he must do another 12 laps, but L12.

The four main items the driver is interested in are:

(a) His position.
(b) His distance to the man in front.
(c) His lead on the man behind.
(d) The number of laps left to be completed.

In some cases, he will also like to know his lap time and to be told of any lap record achieved by himself or another driver. He should also be informed if any of his more dangerous rivals have fallen out of the race.

The first information that should be given is the position. On a short circuit, there is no point in giving this information before the various cars have more or less settled down into their respective positions, that is, after the completion of the third or fourth lap. On a long circuit, however, such as the Nürburgring, this information should already be given at the end of the second lap. Subsequently any change in position should be signalled at once because that is what the driver is most interested in. If the car immediately in front of yours has run away enough to be out of sight, the gap between that car and yours should be given for two consecutive laps, so that you can see at what rate you are losing ground. If the pit manager thinks that, on the grounds of your practice times, you could do better than you actually are doing he might put out a sign giving you your actual lap time. The driver knows best under which circumstances he achieved his best practice laps and he will then be able to judge if he can safely go any faster. There is no point in showing lap times if the track is wet, however, as they lack any basis of comparison.

The driver is also interested to know which is the car in front of his. So instead of showing a board reading '—10', which would mean that he is running 10 seconds behind the car in front, the name of the driver handling that car should be added, to read for instance, '—10 Gurney'. This will help him in his judgement, as previous racing experience or practice will have shown if he can hope to match that particular combination of car and driver or not. If the driver sees that he cannot close the gap between the car in front and his, or if he is out in front of everyone else, he will be more interested in knowing which, and how far, is the next car behind him. Time and again, for instance every five laps, the number of laps left to be run must also be signalled. If, driving as fast as you can, you are closing up at the rate of 1 second a lap on an opponent who has a 30 seconds lead and there are still 30 laps to go, your race tactics will obviously be very different from what they would be if only 7 or 8 laps were left to be done. With no hope of catching your rival before the end, you would then concentrate on keeping your position while nursing the car as much as possible.

Signalling is quite a difficult task because it is not easy for the person in charge of it to know exactly what the driver wants to know at any given moment. So a code should be decided upon by which the driver can ask his pit for the information he is most likely to want. It may be decided that if the driver points forward with his finger, he wants to know how far ahead is the car in front of him; pointing rearward will then mean, 'By how much am I leading the next man?' Turning circles with his finger may be the code for asking how many laps are left to be run, while tapping with a hand on the helmet is the usual sign for informing the pit staff that the driver intends to come into the pits on the following lap, and everything likely to be needed, such as oil, water, fuel, the jack and the more usual tools, should be kept ready.

Most pit managers usually concentrate so much on their own car and the ones immediately in front and behind, that they tend to forget about the general pattern of the race. Here is an example: your car is running, say, in fourth or fifth position, without being seriously challenged. Suddenly one of the leaders makes a short pit stop and rejoins the race three or four positions behind your car and, say, 45 seconds behind on time. This combination of a fast car and fast driver will now probably start lapping very quickly in an endeavour to make up as many places as possible before the end of the race. A good pit manager will immediately become aware of this menace and signal for instance '+45 Moss'; on the next lap, the signal may become '+42 Moss' and the next time round '+39 Moss', thus disregarding all the cars that might find themselves between yours and that of the driver who is coming up fast through the field. Having been informed of the danger in time, you may be able to find just that little extra speed that will reduce the average rate at which your dangerous rival is closing the gap from 3 to 2 seconds and thus keep him at bay until the end of the race. If, using less foresight, your pit manager had waited until this faster driver had come up through the field to occupy the position just behind you before warning you of his presence—when he had closed up to say, 10 seconds—it would probably have been too late for you to take any counter-measures.

Though I believe that, in normal circumstances, the pit signals should give the driver information rather than orders, this is a case where the pit manager should even take the initiative of putting out a faster sign as soon as he has realised the menace, in order to enable his driver to react immediately. But in the following laps, the signals should make it quite clear why the faster signal has been given.

It is useful for the pit manager to know if the driver has actually understood the signal put out to him. As far as possible all signals which have been understood should be acknowledged by a sign. Signals may be missed by a driver because of bad visibility, or because the signal is hidden by another car which is just being passed. The signalling personnel should be aware of such a possibility and should not hesitate, if necessary, to repeat the signal on the next lap if they believe that it has not been clearly understood. In a long-distance race, it is of particular importance that the signal calling the driver in for refuelling is not missed. Many races have been won by stretching the distance between refuelling stops to the utmost, thus saving one stop compared with rival competitors. But this also means that there are only a few drops of fuel left in the tank when the car comes in for refuelling and if the driver misses the 'come-in' signal, his car is in danger of running out of fuel and being put out of the race. It is therefore a wise precautionary measure to signal the refuelling stop twice: two laps before the car is due in, a signal should be put out 'In 2 laps'; next time round, the signal should read 'In' so that if the driver misses one of the signals, he still knows exactly when to stop.

When night driving is involved, such as at Le Mans, in the Rheims 12 hours race, or in some of the races included in the Tour de France, it is essential that the signalling panel should be properly illuminated and also be made readily recognisable by a particular colour or a large-sized sign attached to it. The normal lighting of the pit area is quite insufficient to enable the driver readily to pick out his own signal from the maze of boards being kept ready to be shown to other cars.

THE RACE

The pit organisation having been laid down, all arrangements having been made for accurate timing and signalling, and the race tactics having been decided upon, you can now concentrate on making a good start.

There are two main types of start: one is the so-called Le Mans start, which is often used in Gran Turismo and sports car races though no longer in Britain; the other is the Grand Prix start.

The Le Mans Start

For the Le Mans start, the cars are all lined up, herringbone fashion, with their backs to the pits. The rule is that the engine must be stopped and the doors must be closed. About one minute before the start, the drivers take position in a circle painted on the road, opposite their respective cars. At the starter's signal, everyone runs across the road, jumps into his car and tries to get away as quickly as he can. The goggles should have been properly adjusted about ten seconds before the flag is due to be dropped, but no more, to obviate misting up. Obviously the gear lever should have been left in first gear, so that the only thing the driver has to do, as soon as he has got into his seat, is to depress the clutch pedal, operate the starter and release the clutch as soon as the engine has fired, to get the car off the mark. A combined ignition and starter switch saves valuable time, but if this is not provided, and the car's fuel system incorporates an electric pump that is brought into action by the same switch as the ignition, this should not be left on while the driver is waiting for the flag to fall, because the pump may flood the carburettors and make the engine reluctant to start.

All this sounds very simple, but it is amazing how much time can be saved at the start if the starting procedure is thoroughly rehearsed before the race. Careful timing will show if, with an open car, time is saved by jumping over the door into the cockpit rather than opening the door. Every movement should be studied so that the driver is correctly seated as quickly as possible, and no time is lost in locating the ignition and starter switches. Drivers who jump into their cars without proper

"G. P." LAP CHART

Date__________
Circuit__________ Length__________
Event__________
Car__________ No.__________
1st Driver__________
2nd Driver__________

Air Temp.__________
Weather__________
Tyre Pressure. Front__________
Rear__________
Axle Ratio__________

Existing Lap Record__________
by__________
Fastest practice time__________
by__________

NUMBER OF LAPS

CAR NO.	DRIVERS	POSITION	1	2	3	4	5	6	7	8	9	10	11	12	13	14	15	16	17	18	19	20	21	22	23	24	25
		1																									
		2																									
		3																									
		4																									
		5																									
		6																									
		7																									
		8																									
		9																									
		10																									
		11																									
		12																									
		13																									
		14																									

POSITION	26	27	28	29	30	31	32	33	34	35	36	37	38	39	40	41	42	43	44	45	46	47	48	49	50	51	52	53	54	55	56
1																															
2																															
3																															
4																															
5																															
6																															
7																															
8																															
9																															
10																															
11																															
12																															
13																															
14																															

RACE RESULT:

1st__________
2nd__________
3rd__________

REMARKS:

Fig. 16. A typical lap chart for use by pit staff. Chart-keeping calls for much discipline and concentration

rehearsal have found themselves sitting with one leg going through the steering wheel—hardly the right way of making a fast getaway! And remember that if you do use the door, you can save the time taken to close it, because it will automatically slam itself shut as soon as the car accelerates away.

Of course the most brilliantly performed starting procedure can be marred by an engine that is reluctant to fire. It is therefore absolutely essential to find out the exact throttle opening on which the engine, that has been previously warmed up, starts most readily. And it is equally important that in the excitement of the actual start of the race, the driver keeps his head and strictly adheres to the drill that has been found to give the best results. Sports and Gran Turismo car races for which the Le Mans starting procedure is often used, are usually quite crowded; cars of all capacities run together and a messed-up start may not only mean the loss of a good starting position, but also that one may have to wind one's way through a compact field of slower cars which will delay one's progress while the leaders consolidate their positions.

The Grand Prix Start

For a Grand Prix start the cars are lined up in staggered rows with three cars in the front row, two cars in the second, three cars in the third, and so on. There may of course be more cars per row if the road is wide enough. The positions are usually determined by practice times, the drivers who have put up the best times getting a place in the front row, the next best in the second row and so forth. In most cases, the fastest driver in any given row is placed in the position that will give the inside of the first bend or corner after the start, so as to minimise any possible baulking.

About three minutes before the starting signal is due to be given, all cars should be in position on the starting grid. Between two minutes and one minute to go, the engine, which will have been previously warmed up so that the oil and coolant will have reached their proper working temperatures, should be started. If it is started up earlier (which is usually forbidden by the regulations anyway), it is bound to overheat unduly (unless it is air-cooled), as racing cars do not have a fan to activate the air circulation through the radiator. As soon as the engine is running, give a glance at the instruments to check if everything is working properly. The idling speed should be kept between 3,000 and 4,000 r.p.m. to prevent plug fouling.

If, for any reason, the engine should not start, let everyone know by holding an arm up in the air. This is particularly important, as the other drivers must be informed that you will be unable to move when the starting signal is given, so that they can act accordingly—otherwise a bad mix-up is very likely to happen. According to the current rules, a car is not allowed to start in a race unless the engine has been started up by the self-starter.

If all goes well, everything should be ready when the sign 'one minute to go' appears, while you sit as calmly as possible in the cockpit, watching the instruments and the other cars. Not until the half-minute sign comes up should you adjust your goggles, as otherwise they may mist up, especially if the weather is cool. Only when this has been done should first gear be engaged, as due to the high idling speed of the engine, considerable stress is imposed upon the clutch-release bearing if the clutch is kept disengaged for any length of time. With the start now in sight, the engine speed must be increased to the figure which experience has proved to give the best getaway, which probably lies between 4,000 and 5,500 r.p.m.; the clutch is slowly released to the point where you feel it is just beginning to grip. In order to prevent the car from starting to creep (which may involve a time penalty) you may slightly apply the foot brake by using the heel-and-toe method, or use the hand brake, but a small block of wood, or a stone, about half an inch high, placed in front of a wheel when the car is pushed to the start, provides a much more convenient way of preventing the car from rolling forward too soon.

Down goes the flag and in goes the clutch! This is the moment where very delicate control of the pedals is essential. Clutch slip and wheelspin should keep the engine turning fast enough to provide useful power, but excessive wheelspin will mar the start and excessive clutch slip may burn the clutch. Burnt clutches have lost many races within five seconds of the start.

Even the best of drivers can make a mess of the start. In 1959, when he looked a probable World Champion, Tony Brooks lost all chance of the title when he burnt his clutch on the starting line of the Italian Grand Prix at Monza, in trying to make a lightning getaway. Moss himself has been seen to be left behind on the starting line and quite often back markers who are less in the limelight than front-row starters manage to jump the flag and wind their way through the field to join the leaders. If this happens to you, it gives you a good chance to learn something and also to take advantage of the faster cars' slipstream; but be fair and do not forget to look in your mirror. Faster cars and drivers will soon come up behind you; they have proved during practice that they can lap faster than you can, so there is no point in baulking them and jeopardising their chances of catching up with the better starters. Don't make a nuisance of yourself—let them by as soon as they come up close enough and you see a chance to give way to them. By trying to stay in front of them, you only ruin their chances in the race without any benefit to yourself; on the contrary you will probably get rather nervous and sooner or later make a mistake. But when you have let a faster man pass you, by all means try and stay with him; observe his methods, watch where he brakes and see where his line is different from yours; you will probably finish the race a better driver.

It is also very easy to over-rev the engine during the first few hundred yards following the start. At this stage the cars are proceeding in such close company that but little attention can be devoted to the instruments in general and the rev-counter in particular, while the noise level is so high that it is almost impossible to distinguish the roar of one's own engine from that produced by the other cars. This is why it is not unusual for an excellently prepared car to be retired on the very first lap, due to a bent valve. Such a mistake has occasionally been the lot of even some of the very best drivers, but it is still no excuse for not being extremely careful that it does not happen to you.

In the Race

Apart from trying to save split seconds everywhere he can, of which enough has been said in previous chapters, one of the driver's main problems during the race will have to be faced when other competitors must be overtaken or when a faster car comes up behind.

When two cars and drivers are very nearly equally matched, and are racing neck and neck, there is, of course, no question of the one in front giving way to the other, but it is the duty of the leader to make room for his follower to pass, if he can, whenever it does not bring him off his proper line. For the follower, the only chances to get by his rival are to out-brake him into a corner, to pass him after the corner if he has managed to take the latter a little faster, or by slipstreaming on a straight.

These cases have been dealt with in the 'overtaking' section. The drivers involved in a struggle of this sort always use their mirrors extensively to watch their opponent and know exactly what he is about to do. It is therefore current practice and perfectly safe for the car behind to try to overtake on either side, whichever is the more convenient and safe, except on a straight, where the car in front should keep sufficiently to its right to enable a slipstreaming driver to pass on the left, if he can.

The problem is quite different when the speed differential of the two cars is greater or the drivers are less evenly matched. A driver who knows that he cannot match some of the other competitors in the race—and he *should* know from experience or practice times—should keep an eye on his mirrors every time a long enough straight between two corners provides the opportunity of doing so, and occasionally cast a quick glance over his shoulder at a hairpin (if there is one on the circuit), the better to judge the distance between himself and the cars that may come up behind. A faster car or driver should never be baulked by one who is definitely slower, and a driver who does not bear this in mind is bound to make himself unpopular very soon.

As soon as a faster car has come up sufficiently close to be expected to pass at the first opportunity, you should give way to enable it to pass as easily as possible, even at the cost of a few fractions of a second if you are not terribly pressed yourself. For instance, if the faster driver is coming up just behind at the approach to a corner, you should start slowing down a little earlier than usual, yield the better approach position to the corner, and make it quite clear that you are prepared to let the other car overtake you, eventually signalling the other driver on which side you are going to make room for him.

There is, of course, no point in losing time unnecessarily, and if you see that you can take the bend without getting in the other driver's way you should do so, and make room at the exit of the curve. If it is a right-hand corner which, following the normal line, you will leave close to the left-hand side of the road, you should stay there and signal the driver behind to overtake on the right, and you must not cut across his path again before he can do so. In races in which cars of vastly different performance run together, as is usual in sports or G.T. car events, overtaking can become a major hazard. Down the long straight at Le Mans, for instance, the speed differential between the fastest and the slowest cars may be as much as 60 or 70 m.p.h., and if one of the slower cars pulls out for overtaking when one of the faster cars comes up behind at full speed, a nasty situation may arise. In this case, the driver of the slower car about to pull out is in a better position to judge the speed of the vehicle coming up behind him, than the driver of the faster vehicle is to judge the relative speed of the two slower cars. This is why the driver of a comparatively slow car, who is about to pull out for overtaking—or maybe only to take his correct line through a corner—should be particularly careful and make quite sure that in doing so he does not cut across the line of a much faster vehicle coming up behind. In any case, the driver of the faster car will be extremely grateful for any signal by the driver of the slower car that will inform him of his intentions. If the slower car is closed, and hand signals are not practicable, the driver may use his direction indicators to show that he is aware of the car coming up, for example by flashing his right-hand side indicators, to indicate his intention to stay on the right-hand side of the road.

Flag Marshals

Unfortunately not every driver is a perfect gentleman who is prepared to give way to a fellow-competitor as soon as he is obviously in a position to overtake him. Cases of deliberate baulking are fortunately rather rare; they occur more often in second-rate events in which some drivers take part who have no other means of keeping their opponents at bay. Other inferior drivers are kept so busy by holding their car on the road that they don't seem to have any time left for looking in their mirror.

It is for those who never take a look behind that flag marshals, posted along the circuit, have been provided with a blue flag. "When it is held still, it just draws the attention of the driver who gets it to the fact that he is being followed by another competitor who may wish to overtake him. If the marshal waves the blue flag, the driver is instructed to make room for a faster competitor who is about to overtake him. A driver who feels that he is being baulked by another competitor may appeal to a flag marshal to use his blue flag by waving his hand to draw his attention to the situation.

The use of the blue flag is a much more difficult task than one might think. If the flag is abused, it loses all significance, and drivers cease to take any notice of it. But it must be used when circumstances call for it, otherwise it is just as well to have no flag marshals at all. It is quite difficult for anyone without racing experience to judge when the flag should be given, and when not. A red car is not necessarily faster than the others, and a good flag marshal should not only be fully aware of what is happening in the race, in order to be prepared to show the blue flag at the appropriate moment, but he should also know at first glance who is who and which, of two cars racing in close company, is likely to be the faster one.

Marshals also have other flags at their disposal: the yellow caution flag, the red flag which is very rarely used and calls for a full and immediate stop, and the blue-and-yellow striped oil warning flag. The correct use of the latter also calls for considerable experience, not only in detecting oil left on the track by competing cars, but also in judging if the amount that has been spilled is harmless or warrants the use of the flag. The oil warning flag should be used only in the area made dangerous by the oil, and only for the time necessary for competitors to complete a few laps —just long enough to make sure the drivers remember where the oil is. If it is held out longer than necessary, it will cause confusion and may not be taken seriously if another patch of oil is left on the track at a later stage of the race.

DO'S AND DON'T'S

Do's

Start racing at the lowest possible level so that you can assess your own ability compared with other people's and waste the minimum amount of money if there is little hope of getting anywhere.

If you don't prepare your car yourself, spend as much time as you can with the mechanics who prepare it for you, so as to get as much knowledge as possible of its anatomy. Every car has its weak points, and it is best to know what they are so that you may drive accordingly. It may also help you diagnose any possible abnormality in the car's noise or behaviour during the race, and thus to decide whether to stop or to press on.

Keep an eye on what other people do before the race and an ear open for what they say, particularly if they are more experienced than you are, and look for interesting details of their cars. They may give you useful hints.

If you are your own manager, write down full details of the practice and race conditions: the lap times, fuel consumption, the state of tune of the car, the gear ratios, the tyre pressures, the kind of fuel and oil used, the oil pressure and temperature, the water temperature during the practice runs and the race, and so on and so forth. These notes may be very useful at a later date, especially if you return to the same circuit with the same car or one which is basically similar.

Before you start practising and before the start of the race, make quite sure that someone present in the pits knows your blood group and rhesus.

Wear light, narrow shoes. They will help you to operate the pedals with precision.

When you set off for the race course, for practice or the race itself, always be prepared for any sort of weather. A thunderstorm comes on quickly, and you will be very unhappy if you don't have waterproofs and a visor handy.

If you have to make a Le Mans start, it is worth practising how to get into the car and get it on its way as quickly as possible. It is essential to find out how much the throttle must be opened for a really quick start of the engine, once it has been previously warmed up. Some quite short races are started the 'Le Mans way' these days, and getting off the mark first or tenth may make quite a considerable difference to the results.

Make sure that the driving position is exactly as you want it; especially if the race is a long one, nothing must be neglected to make yourself really comfortable.

Be sure to memorise where the ignition switch is, and which way it must be turned to stop the engine should the throttle fail to shut.

Make quite sure that you can easily identify the instruments and that you know what they should read. If necessary, mark the zone in which the fingers should stand with paint on the dash, so that you can see at first glance if all is well, without having to peer at small figures. This would distract your attention from the road and inevitably ask for trouble or slow you down.

If it rains or is likely to rain, wear leather-backed gloves with which your goggles or visor can be easily wiped or, better still sew a small leather on the back of one of the gloves for this purpose.

If you realise that the engine cannot be started in time for the start of the race, raise your arm up, so that the officials, and above all your fellow-drivers, can see that your car will not move and can take action to avoid ramming it.

If the starting area is not level, put a small stone or a small piece of wood under a wheel to prevent the car from rolling.

It is very easy to over-rev in the first few hundred yards after the start, when you have to watch the other cars running in close attendance rather than the rev-counter and can hardly recognise the sound of your engine from theirs. Take great care that you don't—it may cost you a valve . . . and the race.

During the race, try to drive a little faster than is enjoyable: you cannot go really fast without frightening yourself occasionally.

Pay very careful attention to any oil that may have been left on the track by other cars.

If it starts to rain, slow down sufficiently not to take any risk, then increase speed progressively as you become familiar with the new state of the track.

Watch your rear-view mirrors as often as possible and occasionally have a quick glance behind at a hairpin, so as to judge the distance of your followers more accurately.

Be quite sure you know the meaning of the various flags, and watch for them during the race.

Be quite sure you know the regulations, especially those peculiar to the particular event. It is very important to know the exact starting procedure and the number of people who may work on the car during a pit stop.

Go early to bed the night before the race, and if you feel nervous, don't hesitate to take a sedative in order to get a good night's sleep.

Make an early start to the race. Traffic conditions are likely to be difficult, and having to worry about getting to the start in time will strain your nerves even more than they are before a race anyway.

Make sure you have all the necessary passes to get to the paddock. The arguments that will otherwise ensue will not improve the state of your nerves either.

If you don't know the circuit, try to arrive in time to drive several times round it with a private car before the first practice session starts. This will enable you to take better advantage of the time provided for official practising and you will be less of a nuisance to others who already know their way around. Don't forget to look for possible escape roads during the reconnaissance.

Always wear close-fitting overalls, otherwise the wind will blow them up like balloons and you will feel uncomfortable and look untidy.

Use only two-piece overalls which are much easier to get rid of in case of fire. If possible, have them fire-proofed in a special solution.

From the length of the race and the average speed reached by the fastest cars during practice, calculate the approximate duration of the race. A glance at your watch will then give you a fairly accurate indication of how far the race has progressed. If you are not up amongst the fastest group of competitors, it may also be well worth while calculating how long it will before the leaders are about to lap you, so that you can pay particular attention to keeping out of their way as they close up on you. It's a good way of getting popular with the top men.

Don't's

Don't drink any alcohol with, or after the meal preceding practice or the race, and avoid excessive consumption of alcoholic drinks during the practice and race period.

Don't eat more than a light meal before the race.

Don't forget to carry your competitors' licence with you.

Don't forget to take at least one pair of spare goggles and a visor with you, and to leave them with a reliable person in the pits. If any rain is to be expected, don't forget to treat your goggles and visor with an anti-mist compound. Soap is as good as any of them.

Don't forget to inform your team manager or a reliable person in the pit of your blood group and rhesus: this precaution may save your life in case of an accident.

Don't omit to read the race regulations and make sure you know any rule peculiar to the race concerned.

Don't wait until the last moment to wheel, or drive, your car to its proper starting position.

Don't omit to keep an accurate check on fuel consumption and tyre wear during practice.

Don't wait until the last moment to start the engine.

Don't wait for too long on the starting line with the clutch depressed.

Don't forget properly to adjust your driving mirrors before the start.

Don't pull your goggles down too early: they may mist up.

Don't wear over-warm clothing. Once in the race, you will always get warmer than you had thought. Don't wear waterproofs unless it is raining or likely to rain very hard: otherwise they will be unbearably hot.

Don't forget to tell the people responsible for your signalling what sort of information you will be particularly interested in receiving.

Don't get in the way of faster competitors, but when they have overtaken you, try to keep up with them as long as you can and watch their methods closely: you can learn a lot this way.

Don't take anything a racing driver says for granted. Even the most reliable ones can only say what they *think* they do. If one tells you he takes a bend flat-out with a car similar to yours, and you do not, never try to do what he says without building up progressively to it. If he tells you he brakes at the 200 yards sign for a corner, try first at 300, then 250 and then reduce your distance progressively if you see it really can be done. Drivers usually consider they have reached a landmark when they see it at about 45 degrees to the car's centreline, not when they get level with it, which makes quite a difference. In addition, their instinct of preservation makes them apply the brakes a fraction of a second earlier than they actually think they do.

To do what a racing driver says *he does without building up to it progressively, is the quickest way of getting killed.*

If you decide to change your line through a fast bend, never do so without first trying the new line at a slightly reduced speed, to see if it is really better. It may be worse, in which case, you will be glad you reduced your speed. Only by sheer luck did I avoid a very nasty crash, at about 100 m.p.h., by not observing this rule in one of my first big races.

Don't change gear unnecessarily. Every gear change costs nearly a car's length, so it may be better to stay in a higher gear than to change down to get momentarily better acceleration, and then change up again. In case of doubt, always stay in the higher gear, you will be faster and strain the car less.

Don't drive any faster than is necessary to achieve the best possible result you can hope for, while keeping a reasonable safety margin over the closest competitor. Of course, this can mean driving as fast as you possibly can all the way!

In a long-distance race, never eat anything heavy while waiting for your turn at the wheel, and get as much rest as possible. Before you resume driving, make quite sure of your car's position in the race, and how far in front or behind your most dangerous opponents are.

When handing over to your co-driver, don't forget to inform him of any abnormality in the car that has come to your notice, especially where the brakes are concerned, and also report them to the team or pit manager.

Never wear any item of nylon clothing or clothing of similar material that will melt in the case of a fire.

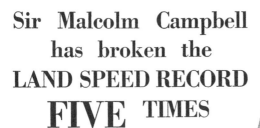

MOTORING SPORTSMEN

SIR MALCOLM CAMPBELL, 'MOTOR SPORT' (1932)

In one season of motor racing a man can experience a great deal. He can be the recipient of all sorts of strange deals from Fortune, enough indeed to provide him with food for thought, and matter for recollection and reminiscence to last for a long time to come.

What, then, of Sir Malcolm Campbell, who, save for a four year interlude of the War, has strenuously engaged himself in pursuit of the sport since 1910? Surely no man alive can equal such a remarkable record, surely few who might have done as much would still be hard at the game after more than twenty years.

When we called at Sir Malcolm's London office we found no jaded veteran contentedly reclining on a heap of well-earned laurels, but a man keen and alert and anxious to gain still further triumphs. In looks and manner Sir Malcolm is essentially a man of action, conveying the impression at once that when he sets out to do a thing he will not be easily deflected from his purpose.

Insatiable.

In our interview, he was not so much inclined to be reminiscent as to discuss his plans for the immediate future, and the possiblilty of Norman Smith bettering his own achievement at Daytona with the "Blue Bird" in 1931. "Smith has got a magnificent car", he said, "and it is five years younger than mine. He ought to do something really good."

"If someone would put up the necessary money I'd like to build a new one to challenge it, but for the present I have to get the 'Blue Bird' prepared. I wish he'd hurry and get things over, because the sand at Daytona is unsafe after the end of March, as the heat softens it."

He mentioned a figure which had been attained in trials substantially above his official speed, so that with the further alterations which have been carried out, the eight-year-old car should still put up a good fight. Miller, he told us, is reported to be building a challenger in America, so there may be another triangular scrap this year.

the attention which has been focused on Campbell's attacks on the World Land Speed Records has rather diverted appreciation of his equally successful career on road and track. In the first 200 Mile race at Brooklands in 1921 he was in the Talbot Darracq team which took the first three places, Seagrave being first and Lee Guinness second. In 1927 he won it in a Bugatti after a great duel with Vernon Balls, and repeated his success the next year on the famous Delage on which Benoist won the British Grand Prix, this time at a speed of 78.3 m.p.h. At Boulogne in 1926 he put up a lap of 70 m.p.h. in practice, but later his engine blew up. Next year, again in a Bugatti, he won at a speed of 67 m.p.h. in pouring rain, his hands being badly cut by the rubbing of the steering wheel. In 1928, in the Boillot Cup, his brakes failed and the car crashed, but the next day, on the Delage, after a terrific duel with Galthier on a Bugatti, won at a speed of 72 m.p.h.

With Bug and Delage.

The same year he drove his Bugatti in the R.A.C. T.T. and was much fancied, but he and Lord Howe were troubled with leaky petrol tanks. In Campbell's case the spirit poured out onto the red-hot exhaust pipe at the first stop, and the car was burnt to a cinder. Next year he put up the record lap at Phoenix Park, and was in the winning team with Caracciola and Lord Howe. He also won the gold star race on the Delage, which was later sold to Lord Howe. The latter repeated the performance in 1931.

We ventured a question or two about his early days at racing, a subject which is always intriguing, especially to those whose introduction to the sport is comparatively recent. "My first real racing car," Campbell said, "was a 60 h.p. Darracq. I bought and ran this in 1910, and in the previous year it had won the Vanderbilt Cup in America." The Darracq was the very first of the "Blue Birds". It was in 1912 that Campbell had one of his numerous close calls: he was driving the Darracq at Brooklands, and when coming down the finishing straight the offside front tyre burst. A moment later the wheel came off, and the rear offside one did likewise! The racer of 1910 with its great ground clearance was a very different proposition from the low-built vehicle of today, but the driver somehow managed to straighten up and skate along the edge of the track. After crossing the finishing line the car spun round and slid sideways, but was somehow brought to rest without overturning. In those days car racing was not the only pastime which attracted Sir Malcolm, and as might be expected from a man of his temperament and calibre, the infant science of aviation gained him as an enthusiastic adherent. Campbell, in fact, can claim to be a real pioneer of flying, for in 1909 he designed and built a monoplane. A 16 h.p. V-twin engine was this craft's power unit, and the whole job of building it occupied six months. Alas for the hopes of its constructor, the aeroplane was not an unqualified success, and save for sundry hops she never really took the air.

The War and the R.F.C.

But later Campbell's aviation aspirations were to be given full scope. Following the outbreak of the war, when he at once joined up and served in France as a motorcycle D.R., Sir Malcolm subsequently transferred to the Royal Flying Corps, and served from 1915 to 1919 as a pilot. Much of his war flying was done as a ferry-pilot – a job full of variety, since one might be called upon to fly a Sopwith "Pup" to France on one day and return with a war-worn F.E. on the next trip home.

"What first turned your attention to breaking World's records?" we asked Sir Malcolm. He confessed he could not remember; anyhow, the idea suddenly came to him. The acquisition of the 100 h.p. Grand Prix Peugeot gave him the chance, and at Brooklands he set up records for the kilometre, mile and five miles. As he was finishing the lap which would have given him the ten mile distance a front tyre burst, and the car took charge. Campbell just managed to keep the car under control after nearly leaving the track, and found that the other tyres were also on the verge of collapse.

About this time the Sunbeam Company had constructed the famous 350 h.p. racer. The engine, it appears ,was built by the famous Sunbeam Company for the R.N.A.S. just before the War, but was never used. Mr Coatalen saw it lying about, and forthwith proceeded to build it into a racing chassis. Lee Guinness put up some records with it at Brooklands, and then Captain Campbell bought it and took it to Saltburn. He had a good run and carried off the record with a speed of 135 m.p.h. The run was not without incident, for a dog crossed the track on his second trip, but happily it got out of the way. This performance had a most diappointing sequel, for the record was only timed by hand, and was disallowed by the Central Board.

The next year Captain Campbell decided to take the Sunbeam to the International Speed Trials at Fanöe (pronounced Fanoo), an island off the west coast of Denmark. When he reached Fanöe he found drivers from all the continental nations there. Refitting the gearbox, which had not been completed before he reached Denmark, took some time, and then on his first run he had trouble with his shock absorbers. However, by working day and night, everything was fixed in time for the races. The Sunbeam put up an average speed of 138 m.p.h., and in the race next day defeated the foreign drivers by a very large margin. Campbell and his crew were naturally delighted at this result, but were once more defeated by the timing apparatus. A proper electric outfir was used on this occasion, and was as accurate as could be made, but it was not approved by the International Body and the record was declared void.

Most people would have been too disgusted to continue, but Campbell is a man who refuses to admit defeat. Next year he took no chances, and brought along with him the R.A.C. timing apparatus, officials and all. The car was properly prepared this time and his hopes were high. Unofrtunately, the weather had been very stormy and the beach was littered with debris of all kinds. He appealed to the authorities to have this cleared away, and also pointed out the danger of letting the crowd of spectators so close to the course. The rubbish was cleared from the sands, but they were still very uneven. Nothing more could be done, so Campbell set off for the start. The car was in excellent form, and was roaring down the measured mile, when suddenly as it was about to cross the finishing strip, the two back tyres came off together, and after a sickening wrench got clear of the wheels, and careered down the course in front of the car. Mercifully, they kept clear of car and the crowd alike, and Campbell, by most amazing skill, managed to keep the car from slewing round and turning over. The cause of the accident was at once apparent. The car was fitted with beaded-edge tyres, which, of course, are only held on by air pressure forcing the beads into the rim. These were changed to wired-edge, and Campbell had another shot. Once again the same thing happened, only this time it was a front tyre. This came off halfway down the measured mile, made straight for the crowd, killed a boy and demolished the timing hut. Meanwhile Campbell was fighting for his own life and that of hundreds of others, for if the car had got out of control it would have gone into the spectators with appalling results. Once again he averted disaster by a narrow margin.

"The authorities were completely to blame for the whole thing," said Sir Malcolm; "it wasn't for want of my telling them."

After these two failures he was more than ever determined to set up the record, and as soon as possible went down to Pendine. Here under the most adverse weather conditions he was successful, and covered the mile at an average speed of 146 m.p.h.

The exploits of the Sunbeam had drawn attention to the kudos attached to the World Speed Record. Sir Malcolm felt that he had reached the highest speed of which the car was capable, and set about designing another car which would do 180 m.p.h, which he calculated would be sufficient for some years to come. This car was the now-famous Blue Bird, and the fact that she attained in 1931 a speed 60 m.p.h. in excess of this shows how well she was designed in the first place.

Of the more recent history which the "Blue Bird" and its great driver have built up there is no need to recount, since it is still fresh in everyone's memory. And now that the car has undergone yet another rejuvenation, we may expect a further chapter to be added in the near future.   (– *Motor Sport* profile, 1932)

ALBERTO ASCARI (1918–1955)

Alberto Ascari is a case for the argument that sporting skill is in the genes. His father Antonio was one of the great drivers of the 1920s but was killed racing an Alfa Romeo in 1925 when son Alberto was only seven years old. Like many before him Ascari started racing on two wheels before having his first taste of cars in 1940, at the wheel of one of Enzo Ferrari's 815 sports cars in that year's Mille Miglia. After the war Ascari drove Maseratis alongside their chief driver Luigi Villoresi, from whom Alberto learnt valuable lessons. Throughout 1947 Ascari's Maserati 4CLT was plagued with mechanical problems. The next few years were better with Ascari racking up a few victories in important events. The best, however, was yet to come. In 1949 he and Villoresi moved to Ferrari and now the wins started to come. In the next season Alberto scored nine victories and in 1951 six. The next season belonged to the young Ascari with a dozen victories that made him world champion. It was a feat he was to repeat the next year. Ascari signed for Lancia for 1954 but as the cars weren't ready until the end of the season he was loaned to other teams. Tragically, Alberto Ascari was killed the next year testing a Ferrari sports car at Monza.

PRINCE BIRABONGSE BHANUBAN (1914–1985)

Entering himself in races under the pseudonym 'Bira', Prince Birabongse was educated at Eton and Cambridge and was the epitome of the gentleman racing driver. Not that Bira was some rich man with more wealth than talent. Far from it. Bira started racing at Brooklands in a Riley Imp in the mid '30s. His cousin Prince Chula Chakrabongse then bought him an ERA R2B which the pair christened 'Romulus'. ERA and Bira were names that would become synonymous. With Prince Chula running their 'White Mouse Stable' Bira scored numerous successes, often against the strongest of opposition. In 1935 he placed Romulus second behind Richard Seaman in another ERA at the Berne GP.

Bira was a very fast and neat driver, almost expressionless in the car, and like his cars was always immaculately turned out.

After the war the stable was back in action with the famous ERAs and also a Maserati 4CL with which he immediately won at Chimay in Belgium. But it was in 1949 that Bira had perhaps his finest season. He was second to Fangio's similar car at the Argentine GP but then beat him in the second heat at the Grand Prix de

Roussillon at Perpignan. To beat Fangio in a straight fight in a similar machine was all one needed to do to prove one's talent. Prince Birabongse Bhanuban of Siam had no shortage of that quality.

RUDOLF CARACCIOLA (1901–1951)

Rudolf Caracciola started racing in 1922 with a Fafnir but very soon after joined the Mercedes-Benz team, with which he was to stay for virtually all of his career. Initially successful at hillclimbs and sprints, Caracciola won his first grand prix at the Automobil-Verkehrs- und Übungs-Straße (AVUS) track in the 1926 German Grand Prix. The next year the famous Nürburgring track was opened and Caracciola won the sports car race there. The following year he won his home grand prix again and also won the Tourist Trophy sports car race in Ulster, which had been held in foul conditions. Incredible drives in adverse conditions became a Caracciola trademark gaining him the nickname 'Regenmeister' or rain-master.

In 1931 Mercedes temporarily retired from racing and Caracciola briefly joined Alfa Romeo. He had a very successful few seasons with the Italian team until he had a serious accident practicing for the 1933 Monaco GP. Weeks later his wife was killed in a skiing accident; Caracciola took time to recover from his physical injuries combined with the mental anguish of his loss. In 1934 a now fit Caracciola re-joined the new Mercedes team. Their first season was slightly disappointing but the next year Caracciola won six grands prix. Rudolf Caracciola was now to play an active and successful part in the legendary seasons of the Silver Arrows, winning numerous events in his Mercedes-Benz racers and becoming European champion. Caracciola was also writing his name into the record books with several speed records that included a 267mph run in the 5.0–8.0-litre class.

JUAN MANUEL FANGIO (1911–1995)

In debates about who is the greatest Formula One driver of all time the name Juan Manuel Fangio is always mentioned. Born in Buenos Aires, the Argentinian started his motor racing career in the long distance races held in South America in the 1930s and 1940s over terrible roads, covering over 1,000 kilometres or more. For example, the Grand Prix de Norte, which Fangio won in a Chevrolet, was a gruelling 5,900 miles long. Fangio was 37 years-old when he arrived in Europe in 1948 with a Maserati 4CLT but age did not hinder his progress. His first full European season in 1949 brought numerous victories and attracted the attention of the European factories, especially Alfa Romeo who signed him up for the 1950 season. The Italian company was not to regret its choice, as Fangio came second to Farina in the world championhip. The next year nothing got in his way and Fangio became world champion, scoring 31 points out of a possible 36. In 1952 Fangio drove several different machines but a serious accident at Monza ruined his season.

A second world championship came Fangio's way in 1954 with victories in Maseratis and, towards the end of the season, Mercedes-Benz cars. The Argentinian stayed with Mercedes for 1955 and won his third world championship. However, after the Le Mans disaster Mercedes withdrew from racing and Fangio was once again without a car. Ferrari beckoned and Fangio took the Ferrari-Lancia D50 to his fourth championship. In 1957 Fangio returned to Maserati and won his fifth and last championship before retiring at the end of the next season.

Juan Fangio had not only skill behind the wheel, but also apparently unlimited powers of concentration and stamina that were the envy of drivers young enough to be his sons. He also had incredible car control and was able to drive consistently at the limit and even beyond it.

GIUSEPPE FARINA (1906–1966)

Guiseppe Farina was the classic fiery Italian, given to emotional outbursts and displays of temperament that sometimes got in the way of victories for this otherwise stylish and highly skilled driver. Farina came under the wing of his friend and mentor Tazio Nuvolari in the early '30s and posted good results in Alfa Romeos in the 1933 and '34 seasons. Farina drove privately-entered Maseratis and then Alfa Romeos for Scuderia Ferrari before joining the newly emergent Alfa Romeo works team in 1937. Farina continued driving for Alfa, continuing into 1940 and winning the Tripoli GP in a Tipo 158. Farina took up the same car after the war, winning the 1946 GP des Nations in Geneva. The best was yet to come, however. After a season in Maseratis in 1949 Farina re-joined Alfa Romeo and took the 158 to victory in the first ever British F1 Grand Prix at Silverstone. Subsequent victories at the Italian, Swiss and Bari Grands Prix secured the first ever F1 championship.

The season proved to be the highlight of Farina's career. In the following seasons he was involved in several serious accidents, including a fiery crash in a Ferrari sports car while practising for a 1,000km race. Farina raced again, but a full recovery from his injuries took a long time and the Italian finally had to retire from the sport he loved so much at the end of 1955.

STIRLING MOSS (1929–)

It is to pay Stirling Moss a great disservice to remember him as the greatest driver never to win the world championship, even though it is probably true. Moss started racing when he was only 18 in a Cooper-Jap Formula 3 car in 1948 and immediately proved that he was a winner. The next year he moved on to larger cars and won the Tourist Trophy in a Jaguar XK120. Over the next few years Stirling honed his skills, winning rallies and circuit races in both single-seaters and sports cars. Unsurprisingly he caught the eye of Enzo Ferrari, who offered him the chance of glory in one of his cars. Moss, however, was deeply patriotic and decided that he had to drive a British car. Eventually though, he swallowed his national pride and equipped himself with a Maserati 250F for the 1954 season, joining the works team halfway through the year. Mercedes-Benz team manager Alfred Neubauer was impressed enough with his performances to offer Moss a drive alongside Fangio in his team. With the master Fangio as teacher Moss's skill and talent increased still further. Wins came in the Mille Miglia, Targa Florio, Tourist Trophy and the British Grand Prix. He finished the season as runner-up to Fangio in the F1 championship. After Mercedes withdrew Moss went back to a Maserati 250F and was runner- up again – as he was in 1957, 1958 and 1960. One victory that meant an enormous amount was his triumph at the 1956 British GP at Aintree in a Vanwall. A win for a British driver in a British car at the British Grand Prix was a good day's work for the patriotic Moss.

He finished his racing career in a Lotus; a career that was cut short by an accident at Goodwood. The precise cause was never discovered but head injuries robbed Moss of the sharp powers of judgement, concentration and skill that had put him above almost everyone else.

FELICE NAZZARO (1881–1940)

Born a few years before Karl Benz produced his first car, Felice Nazzaro was one of the pioneers of motor racing at the beginning of the 20th century. His name was synonymous with FIAT, being associated with the Turin-based company for almost all of his life. This son of a coal-miner served an engineering apprenticeship with the company and his skill as a mechanic and driver was immediately recognised. Nazzaro's first race for FIAT was in the 1900 Vicenza-Padua race in which he came third. The next year he won the Giro d'Italia in one of the firm's first four-cylinder cars. By 1905 FIAT was heavily involved in racing and Nazzaro became a works driver alongside Vicenzo Lancia. Lancia was a quick driver but tended to get carried away, which often resulted in machine failure whereas Nazzaro was a steadier pair of hands and tended to finish races. This happened in the Gordon Bennett race in 1905 in which Lancia retired early while the more restrained man finished a creditable 2nd.

Like Lancia, Nazzaro ventured into building his own machines but was unable to match his former team-mate's success. He gave up his automotive business in 1916 and raced after the war in the '20s in various FIAT cars, notching up many successes including wins in GPs. After a long career behind the wheel Nazzaro eventually retired to take up a position as competitions manager at FIAT.

TAZIO NUVOLARI (1892–1953)

In many experts' eyes, Tazio Nuvolari was the greatest racing driver of all time. Certainly his character, personality and courage fitted the template for such an accolade. Nuvolari started racing motorcycles and even in those early days he had a reputation for never giving up, even if the machine was wholly unsuitable or failing on him. In 1925 he was given a trial in an Alfa Romeo P2 at Monza but crashed heavily due to a seized gearbox. A week later he was lifted, heavily bandaged, onto his Bianchi motorcyle and won a grand prix. Nuvolari came from a landowning family in Mantua, northern Italy, and by selling some of his land in 1927 was able to set up a team running Bugatti Type 35s. He had numerous victories in the cars but it was in Alfa Romeos in the 1930s that Nuvolari really stamped his mark. Wins were too numerous to list here, but simple numbers don't really tell the whole story of this amazing sportsman. Nuvolari liked to sit high up in his cars and almost danced in the cockpit, jigglijng from side to side while pulling faces. His signature technique was to thunder into a corner and throw the car sideways into a four-wheel slide. It certainly worked.

Nuvolari's most famous victory came in the 1935 German GP when in a vastly inferior Alfa Romeo P3 he beat off all the Silver Arrows to take victory 2min 14.4sec ahead of the second-placed Auto Union. Nuvolari later drove for Auto Union in the 1938 and 1939 seasons, winning several GPs including his fabulous victory in the

1938 British Grand Prix at Donington.

The great Tazio suffered from ill health after the war and had his last race at the age of 58 in a 1.5-litre Cisistalia. Naturally, he won his class.

JOHN RHODES COBB (1899–1952)

John Cobb grew up near the famous Brooklands circuit and caught the bug from watching racing there as a young boy . Cobb's forté would be wrestling the giant cars of the day, and indeed he started his driving apprenticeship in a 1911 10-litre FIAT. His first victory in this behemoth came in 1925 at the West Essex motor club meeting. The next year Cobb drove Parry Thomas's Liberty aero-engined 'Babs' on its first appearance at Brooklands. In 1929 Cobb bought a 10.5-litre Delage and started winning regularly and breaking lap records. One record, the outright outer circuit lap record at Brooklands of 133.88mph, will never be broken.

Despite numerous race wins in circuit racing, many in smaller cars, it is for breaking land speed records that Cobb is more famous. Cobb had Reid Railton design him a record-breaker using two Napier Lion aero engines, with which its driver took the land speed record to 350.20mph in 1938. Cobb then raised this to 369.70mph just before war broke out in 1939. After the war he returned to the challenge and raised the record to 394.19mph, in the process becoming the first man to exceed 400mph. Sadly, in a tragedy that would be echoed by the death of Donald Campbell fifteen years later, Cobb turned to water speed record attempts and was killed at Loch Ness in 1952 in his jet-powered boat.

RICHARD SEAMAN (1913–1939)

Seaman was the typical well-educated and wealthy amateur racing driver. However, unlike many others of the type, he was extremely determined. His career started in earnest in 1934 after he'd left Cambridge. His machine was an MG Magnette with which he had some good drives both at home and abroad. For the next season the by-now professional Seaman took the plunge and bought a new ERA. Unfortunately the expensive new racer proved to be unreliable and, worse still, its manufacturer somewhat unhelpful. Seaman then made the rather eccentric move of buying an old 1927 Delage, which he had his mechanic Guilio Ramponi completely rebuild. Once stripped-down and lightened, the machine proved to be a real giant killer and Seaman's perseverance and skill with the car was noticed by

Mercedes team boss Alfred Neubauer. In 1937 Richard Seaman became the sole British member of the Silver Arrows. He soon mastered the immensely powerful Mercedes but victory would have to wait a year. It came in the German Grand Prix at the Nürburgring. Not surprisingly it became increasingly awkward for an Englishman to drive in a Nazi-supported team but Seaman was advised to continue for diplomatic reasons. Tragically he was killed at Spa in the 1939 Belgian Grand Prix while leading in wet conditions.

ACHILLE VARZI (1904–1948)

It was unfortunate for Achille Varzi that he was born at the same time as his friend and great rival Tazio Nuvolari, for he just lacked the touch of eccentric flair that marks true genius and which would have given him equal talent to Nuvolari. Like Nuvolari, Varzi came from a prosperous family and also raced motorcycles, though surprisingly, although they were racing at the same time, they never did battle on two wheels together. Varzi joined together with his friend and drove one of the Bugatti T35s, but after coming second to Nuvolari in a few races realised that he would be held back if he didn't go it alone. Plan B was to buy a P2 from Alfa Romeo and drive that solo. It was a sound move as Varzi had many successes with the very competitive P2, including victory in the Targa Florio.

There was an opportunity to join the Alfa Romeo team but as Nuvolari was already a member, Varzi decided instead to go to Maserati. Constant manoeuvring in a desire not to compromise each other was a constant feature of the two Italians' careers. In 1934 Varzi went back to Alfa Romeo with the Scuderia Ferrari and had enormous success with the P3 model, winning seven GPs and the Mille Miglia. In 1935 Varzi joined Auto Union and won his first race in the challenging car.

Achille Varzi was a complicated character. He missed the early part of the 1937 due to what was rumoured to be 'an affair of the heart'. Varzi was also known to use drugs. Post-war he rejoined Alfa Romeo, driving the dominant 158 model. Tragically, Varzi was killed in the European GP at Berne when his car skidded on the wet circuit and overturned. The fact that Varzi was not wearing a helmet prompted the FIA to make the wearing of them compulsory thereafter.

FAST LADIES

ELIZABETH JUNEK (1900–1994)

Elizabeth Junek is probably the greatest of all female racing drivers. She started her career competing in her native Czechoslovakia, aided by her loyal husband. In 1926 she moved further afield, entering the Klausen hillclimb in Switzerland. The next year the Juneks attempted something far more ambitious: the gruelling and immensely challenging Targa Florio. The couple arrived a month before the race to prepare and learn the 67 mile-long circuit, even walking it on foot. In the race Elizabeth finished the first lap in fourth place behind the works Bugattis. A problem with her Bugatti's steering forced her to retire, but she had certainly made an impact. When the Juneks returned the next year, Elizabeth was once again fourth at the end of the first lap but on the second she led the field – one of the drivers trailing her was the great Tazio Nuvolari. On the third and fourth laps she fell back to second and then due to mechanical problems finally finished the race in fifth place. It was an outstanding performance. Tragically her husband was killed in the German GP two months later and Elizabeth Junek retired from racing.

KAY PETRE (1903–1994)

Born Kathleen Coad Defries in Toronto, Canada, Petre came to England and married the aviator Henry Petre. Petre bought his new wife a Wolsey Hornet Special for racing but the 4'10" lady soon became famous for driving something rather more challenging: a 10.5-litre Delage. She used this car to battle for the women's outer circuit lap record at Brooklands, raising it to 129.58mph in 1934, only to lose it the next year to another very talented driver called Gwenda Stewart. The two women fought for the record, until Stewart finally triumphed with a speed of 135.95mph.

But Petre was more than just a record breaker. In the early 1930s she took part in all the important events of the motorsport calendar, partnering stars such as Prince Bira and 'Doc' Benjafield. In 1937 Petre went to South Africa and drove in three grands prix, finishing sixth in the Cape Town GP. Sadly her career was cut short by a catastrophic accident at Brooklands when another driver spun and collided with her works Austin.

CARS AND MARQUES

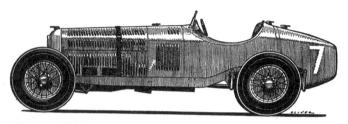

Alfa Romeo, 1932: Europe's first Grand Prix single-seater, the famous Type B monoposto, often referred to unofficially as the P3. In its original 2.6 litre, and subsequent 2.9 litre forms, this superb machine won over forty Continental races between 1932 and 1935.

ALFA ROMEO

Alfa Romeo started life simply as ALFA (Anonima Lomdarda Fabbrica Automobili) just outside Milan in 1910. The new Alfa cars were big and powerful, which is what was required for Italian roads and the size of the country. Alfa's bosses did not dawdle when it came to proving their cars in competition and in 1911 entered a team in the Targa Florio in Sicily. There was no fairytale win first time out, but in 1913 an Alfa came second in the important Parma–Pogio de Berceto hill climb.

In 1915 ALFA became part of Nicola Romeo's industrial empire and Alfa Romeo was born. In 1920 a young Italian called Enzo Ferrari came second in the Targa Florio driving a 20/30hp Alfa Romeo. In 1923 a new engineer joined the company from FIAT. His name was Vittorio Jano and as one of the most talented designers in the world he really put Alfa Romeo on the map. Or more to the point, into the winner's circle. Within a few months of starting his new job Jano had designed an eight-cylinder supercharged 2.0-litre engine and fitted it to the new Alfa Romeo P2 racer. The new car immediately won the first race it entered, the French GP at Lyon. In 1925 the P2 was even more successful, notching up several victories in grand prix events, and driver Count Gaston Brilli-Beri finishing the year with the title of World Champion driver. Subsequently the Alfa Romeo badge was surrounded by a laurel wreath.

Alfa Romeo scored many victories at the end of the decade with its 1500 and 1750 sports models, including victory in the second ever Mille Miglia race in 1928. The P2 was succeeded by the P3 in 1932. Sports car race victories continued to mount up in the 1930s while the GP Alfas faced tougher and tougher competition from rival machines manufactured by Mercedes and Auto Union.

Post-war, Alfa Romeo virtually dominated grand prix racing from 1946 to 1950, winning the first official F1 championship with the fabulous pre-war Type 158 with its 1500cc eight-cylinder engine. For the 1951 season Alfa Romeo built the Type 159 with the same engine but in supercharged form, producing 404bhp. The brilliant Juan Fangio won the championship for Alfa. It was to be the great company's last year in F1, subsequently focusing on sports and saloon car racing.

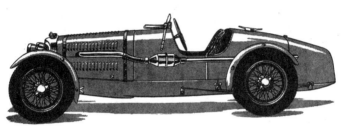

Aston Martin, 1935: the rugged, shapely 1½-litre Aston Martin in 1935 'Ulster' form.

ASTON MARTIN

Aston Martin was founded by Robert Bamford and Lionel Martin in 1914. And the Aston part of the name? That came from the Aston hillclimb in Aston Clinton in Buckinghamshire. The first true Aston Martin car was built in 1919 and won a gold medal in the London–Edinburgh Trial.

By 1921 Lionel Martin and others were regularly winning races at Brooklands. In 1928 Aston Martin went to Le Mans with a pair of its new cars powered by 1.5-litre 63bhp engines designed by the Italian engineer A.C. Bertelli. Both cars retired from the race but the team persevered at the famous French race and from 1931 was to enter the race every year it was held until 1964. Aston Martins continued to race in events all over Europe including the Mille Miglia and the Tourist Trophy, which was usually held on the Ards road course in Northern Ireland.

After the war the company was bought by David Brown and in 1950 Aston Martin started serious racing again with a team of DB2 saloon cars. The cars did well in their class at Le Mans and won their class at the 1952 Mille Miglia.

The company's finest hour, however, was in 1959 when at last an Aston Martin won Le Mans outright with the DBR1 driven by Roy Salvadori and the Texan Carroll Shelby. In the same year Aston Martin built a Formula One car with a 2.5-litre six-cylinder engine based on the sports car unit. After a promising start to the season the cars struggled and never again did Aston Martin attempt F1.

Auto Union, 1936-7: produced for the 750kg Formula, this highly unconventional German car had its sixteen-cylinder engine of over 6 litres installed behind the driver. Although it gained numerous successes, the Auto Union was a notably difficult car to handle.

AUTO UNION

Auto Union was founded in 1932 by a fusion of Horch, Audi, DKW and Wanderer. Auto Union has gone down in history as the inventor of the rear-engined racing car. Today every Formula One car has its engine in the back, but in 1934 Auto Union's designer Dr Ferdinand Porsche was considered to be going out on a limb with his radical design.

The first car was designed to fit the new sub-750kg formula and was powered by a 4.4-litre supercharged V-16 engine that produced around 295bhp. The car caused a sensation on its debut when driver Hans Stuck averaged 134mph around the AVUS circuit during attempts at world speed records. Then the new A-Type went racing proper. It secured a third place at the AVUS GP, a second at the Eifelrennen at the Nürburgring, retired at the next event and then won the remaining three.

The new B-Type for 1935 had a new 4.9-litre engine but was overall a bit of a disappointment, despite a few wins. The next year, however, it all came good with the new 520bhp 6.1-litre C-Type. Victories came thick and fast in both the 1936 and '37 seasons, including a win in the Donington Grand Prix in England. For 1938 the rules changed, with the engine capacity capped at 3.0-litres. This new car, the D-Type, continued Auto Union's success until the war started. With the Zwickau factory ending up in the Russian-controlled zone after the war, that was the end.

Bentley, 1934: John Duff's 3-litre Bentley, winner of the Le Mans 24-hour race in 1924.

BENTLEY

W.O. Bentley's 3-litre four-cylinder model was exhibited at the 1919 London Motor Show but it wasn't until 1921 that the first customer received his car. In May that year Frank Clement took his Bentley to Brooklands and won his race at an average speed of 72.5mph. Bentley had arrived. The next year cars were prepared for the Indianapolis 500 and the Tourist Trophy in the Isle of Man. W.O. Bentley himself came fourth with Frank Clement finishing ahead in second place.

But it was at Le Mans that Bentley's fame was forged. In 1923 a car was entered privately and driven to fourth place by John Duff. The next year, however, Bentley did it properly with a works team of two cars. Duff was back again and with co-driver Frank Clement won the race. It was a cracking start, but unfortunately the team wasn't as successful for the next couple of years, with both cars retiring in the 1925 and '26 races. Happily normal service resumed with Bentley victories in the following two years, although that was nothing to what happened in the 1929 Le

Mans. Equipped with a new 6,597cc Speed-Six model and 4½-litre cars the works Bentley cars took the first four places in the race (a Speed-Six won, followed by three 4½-litre models). The 1930 Le Mans was Bentley's last appearance as a works team and happily victory again went to the Crewe company.

Cooper, 1949: with neat, practical little machines such as this, Formula III thrived in Britain. The Cooper's single-cylinder power units were installed behind the driver's seat.

COOPER

Charles Cooper had worked as a racing mechanic for driver Kaye Don between the wars but in 1946 he built a couple of 500cc racing cars for his son John (father of the Mini Cooper) and a driver called Eric Brandon. They were immediately winners, so in 1948 twelve Mk2s were made, one going to young newcomer Stirling Moss. In 1952 Cooper built a new car with a 2.0-litre Bristol engine, which was also successful.

But Cooper really put itself on the map when its Formula Two cars were a great success in the last few years of the decade, driven by Jack Brabham, Bruce McLaren and Roy Salvadori. Like the pre-war Auto Unions, Coopers were mid-engined whereas all of their rivals built traditional front-engined single-seaters.

Those rivals were forced to think again when Jack Brabham won the F1 world championship in 1959 and then repeated the feat the next year. As the 1960s started, all Formula One cars would be rear-engined. Cooper itself never found its 1950s form again, struggling to find suitable engines to use in the 1960s and then disappearing from racing completely at the end of the decade, leaving its famous name only on the Mini.

Delage, 1925: with a V12, twin o.h.c. two-litre supercharged engine giving 190 b.h.p., the Delage won the French and Spanish Grands Prix of 1925.

DELAGE

L ouis Delage was one of the first drivers to build his own racers. His first machine, fitted with a single-cylinder De Dion engine, came second in the 1906 Coupe de l'Auto race. The De Dion was used up until the end of the first decade of the twentieth century, after which Delage started making his own engines. And sophisticated pieces of machinery they were, too. In 1914 Delage's Grand Prix machines had 4.5-litre engines with double camshafts, desmodromic valves and twin-carburettors. The cars also had four-wheel brakes and five-speed gearboxes – both highly unusual in their day. After the Great War Delage concentrated on sprints and hillclimbs rather than circuit races. One car built for sprinting was a V12-engined machine displacing an immense 10,688cc. As well as achieving success in sprints, this monster also snatched the land speed record when Rene Thomas drove the car to 143.29mph in 1924.

A year earlier a new Grand Prix car had been built, powered by a 2.0-litre V12 engine producing 105bhp. In 1925 two superchargers were added to the engine which brought the power up to 190bhp. These new Delages were formidable competitors and gave the Alfa Romeos a run for their money in the European GPs. Alfa Romeo missed the 1925 Spanish GP and Delage had a magnificent 1-2-3 finish.

Delage himself retired from driving in 1928 but his cars carried on for another eight years. In 1935 the firm merged with Delahaye. Richard Seaman claimed a number of successes in 1936 and it was this that attracted Mercedes-Benz to him.

Delage also built sports cars and in 1939 one finished second at Le Mans, a feat repeated after the war in 1949 when Delage was again robbed of a win, this time by a Ferrari rather than by a Bugatti. It proved to be a sunset result for the French company, which then faded away.

E.R.A., 1935: the British six-cylinder 1½ litre B type E.R.A. gained many international successes in the 'Voiturette' class between 1935 and 1938. After the war, examples were raced against more modern Continental opposition in Grand Prix events.

ERA

ERA stands for English Racing Automobiles. It is fitting that this patriotically-named marque did a fine job of flying the Union Jack at a time when British-made racing cars were very much absent from the winners' circle. ERA, which had been founded in 1933 by driver Raymond Mays, Humphry Cook and Peter Berthon, specialised in building cars for the Voiturette class and never let itself get sidetracked into building road cars. The basic ERA B-type was offered with a supercharged 1.5-litre six-cylinder design based on a Riley engine but customers could also opt for a 1.1-litre version or a 2.0-litre powered model. Only 17 of these 'basic' models were built, but they scored successes all around the world. Prince Chula of Siam's chassis number R2B (nicknamed 'Romulus' – his other ERA was called 'Remus') scored 10 first places, eight seconds and five third places up until the outbreak of the Second World War. In 1936 the little 1.5-litre ERAs took on Maserati and Delage at Monaco and filled four of the first five places in the race.

ERA's peak was in 1937, when its C-type model took to the track. Essentially a B-type but fitted with Porsche-designed rear trailing arms, independent front suspension and hydraulic brakes, the C-type ERA won all over Europe and in no better style than in the Isle of Man where ERAs beat the Maseratis with a resounding 1-2-3-4-5 procession to the flag.

Unfortunately, towards the end of the 1930s ERA began to run short of money and was unable to maintain its momentum. That wasn't the end of the ERA story, however. Post-war the small British cars continued to win, punching above their weight with victories in the Ulster and British Empire Trophy races. New owners in the 1940s carried on experimenting with more modern designs but it is the original B-type that is best remembered. Almost all the original cars survive and are often raced – and often win – in historic motor racing events.

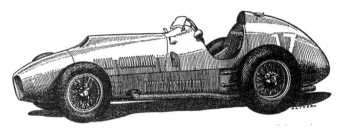

Ferrari, 1951: the Lampredi-designed twelve-cylinder unsupercharged car which broke the Alfa Romeo grip on Formula 1 racing. This particular machine, with carburetter tunnel on the bonnet, was prepared for the 1952 Indianapolis 500 miles race.

FERRARI

Enzo Ferrari had already had a long career as a driver and team manager before he built the first car that carried his name, in 1946. That first car was powered by a 1.5-litre V12 engine and was called the 125 (125 referred to the cubic capacity of each cylinder – 12x125cc=1,500cc). It was available as a sports car with a full-width body or with cycle wings. In 1948 a single-seat version was launched, with a supercharged version of the same engine producing 225bhp. It was Grand Prix racing that was Ferrari's ultimate ambition and his first win came in the same year at Garda, in a 125 driven by Giuseppe Farina. Alfa Romeo, a team that Ferrari had managed in the 1930s, were his toughest adversary. In 1949 Ferrari decided to change from a 1.5-litre supercharged engine to a larger unsupercharged engine designed by Aurelio Lampredi. In 1951 Ferrari at last beat Alfa Romeo fair and square when Froilan Gonzalez won the British Grand Prix at Silverstone in his Ferrari 375.

It was to mark the start of an incredible career for this most famous of all racing marques. Formula One remained Enzo Ferrari's prime fascination and goal, but Ferraris would also compete throughout the 1950s and '60s in sports car racing; winning Le Mans in 1960 with the 250 Testa Rossa. The factory itself ran the F1 team while privately-owned teams were given the task of entering and winning with the sports cars. In 1969 Ferrari became part of the FIAT empire, but was still run in a patriarchal style by its enigmatic founder.

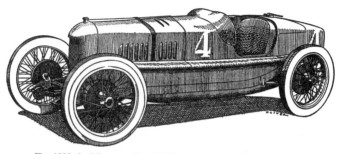

Fiat, 1922: the 2-litre car with which Nazzaro won the French Grand Prix at Strasbourg. With its low, compact build and six-cylinder, roller-bearing engine, it set new design fashions. A similar car won the 1922 Grand Prix of Italy at Monza.

FIAT

FIAT was one of the pioneers of motoring and, like all the manufacturers, wanted to prove its machines in competition. It was also the first Italian manufacturer to make any impression and achieve success outside of Italy. In 1900 its drivers Felice Nazzaro and Vicenzo Lancia (whose own company would one day be owned by FIAT) came first and second in the Padua–Padua race. One thinks of FIATs as small cars with tiny engines, but the early FIAT racers were far from it. For the 1904 Gordon Bennett trophy FIAT had a team of three 14,112cc-engined cars. Unfortunately driver Lancia could do no better than an eighth place in the event. The next year FIAT was back at the same race with 16-litre engines and this time Lancia led the race before retiring, leaving Nazzaro to come second.

The 1907 season was a spectacular one for the northern Italian company with wins at the Targa Florio (the first year the race was held) and the Kaiserpreis in Germany, as well as a grand prix.

One of the best-known FIAT racing cars was 'Mephistopheles', a behemoth of a machine powered initially by an 18-litre aero engine. Nazzaro took this monster to Brooklands in 1908 and had a famous match race against Frank Newton's Napier. Nazzaro beat the British machine with an incredible 121.64mph lap. In 1924 British driver Ernest Eldridge acquired 'Mephistopheles' and fitted it with a 21-litre FIAT airship engine. With it Eldridge raised the world land speed record to an impressive 146.01mph.

Meanwhile FIAT itself built and raced cars that competed in grand prix events throughout the early twenties, often with great success. The factory gradually retired from racing as a proper team, but FIAT cars themselves were still commonplace. The cheapest way to go racing in Italy was to buy a FIAT road car and tune it. Many did so and FIATs competed successfully in epic events like the Mille Miglia and Monte Carlo rally.

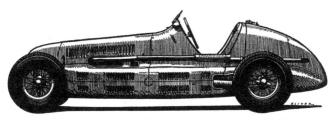

Maserati, 1939-47: the supercharged, four-cylinder 16-valve, 1 ½ litre 4CL Maserati was designed as a 'voiturette', in which class it proved very successful. It subsequently gained numerous Grand Prix successes when its compatriot Alfa Romeos were not competing.

MASERATI

Maserati was founded by three brothers from Bologna and in the beginning was essentially a tuning company, which specialised in improving other makers' cars. One such customer was Diatto. Maserati brother Alfieri had driven Diatto cars in a few events himself and showed their potential. When Diatto stopped racing in 1926 the brothers decided to take over the latest Diatto design and develop it further. The first true Maserati racing car was the Tipo 26, a 1.5-litre eight cylinder-engined machine that Alfieri used to win his class and finish ninth overall in the 1927 Targa Florio. It was a good start that did not go unnoticed by private racers, who flocked to buy their own Maseratis. It was a pattern that continued, with Maseratis always finding favour with private racing teams and individual drivers.

By 1929 Maserati had a 1,078cc supercharged model called the 8C-1100 and a more dramatic V16-engined car (essentially two of the same 8-cylinder engines mounted on a common crankcase) called the V-4. Unlike the Tipo 26 the V-4 wasn't an overnight success and had to wait a year for its first proper victory in the 1930 Tripoli GP. In the same year Maserati formed its first works team and contested Europe's premier events with some success. During the year the first four-cylinder model was produced, called the 4C-1100 (four cylinders, 1100cc).

Maserati couldn't match the resources of the German teams during the 1930s or that of Alfa Romeo, and contented itself by competing in lesser events in Europe and particularly in Britain, again with privateers favouring the Bologna cars.

After the war Maserati moved from Bologna to Modena and was sold to Orsi. In 1946 the pre-war 4CLT returned to the circuit. Under Orsi true Maserati sports cars were built (pre-war cars tended to be converted single-seaters) and were successful in events such as the Mille Miglia. In 1954 Maserati unveiled what is considered to be one of the most beautiful racing cars of all time, the 250F Grand Prix car. The 2.5-litre car was driven to victory by Fangio in the Argentinian and Belgian Grands Prix. The next year Fangio left for Ferrari and Stirling Moss ran his own 250F, winning at Monaco and finishing second to Fangio in the championship.

Mercedes-Benz, 1937: the most powerful Grand Prix car ever built. Its 5.6-litre
engine gave an output of well over 600 b.h.p. The Type W125 won the Tripoli,
German, Monaco, Swiss, Italian and Czechoslovakian Grands Prix of 1937.

MERCEDES-BENZ

Mercedes-Benz was formed in 1926 after the merger of the Daimler and Benz companies. At the time Mercedes was concentrating on sports car racing with its supercharged 6.8-litre S model. The cars, painted in the German white racing colours, looked stunning and formidable, especially the SSK models. Factory driver Rudolf Carraciola almost won the 1929 Monaco GP but his SSK had a ferocious appetite for tyres and his extra stops gave Bugatti the victory with the Mercedes coming in third.

Without doubt the most memorable decade for Mercedes-Benz was the 1930s, with the introduction of the dramatic 750kg formula and the era of the Silver

Arrows. From the start of the formula in 1934 until the outbreak of war, Mercedes battled with rivals Auto Union on Europe's premier race circuits. The ultimate in power and drama was the 1937 W125 machine. The car was fitted with a supercharged 5.8-litre engine that produced an incredible 646bhp. If the W125 accelerated at 150mph on a dry track the rear tyres would spin. The skill required to keep one on a wet track was immense, as was a W125 driver's courage.

Mercedes-Benz emerged from the Second World War a devastated company but gradually rebuilt itself round and by the start of the 1950s was once again a force to be reckoned with. A dream team of Stirling Moss and Juan Fangio drove the works W196 Formula One cars and the company's 300SLRs. In 1955 Moss drove an SLR to an incredible victory at that year's Mille Miglia. However, after its involvement in the tragic Le Mans disaster in the same year Mercedes-Benz withdrew from racing for the best part of three decades.

M.G., 1933: the supercharged 1100 c.c. K3 Magnette won numerous road and track races and sports-car events.

MG

Although MG (which stands for Morris Garages) is always associated with motor racing, the company was rarely in a position to run a fully-fledged works team. Its role was to build sports cars that customers could purchase and then compete in themselves. Even the pure racing models were listed in the Morris Garages catalogue and buyers could count on a level of support from the works until the competitions department was closed in 1935.

MG's first racing victory came in 1927 when a side-valve engined 1802cc tourer won an event in Buenos Aires. In 1928 two new models appeared; the first an 848cc model called the Midget and the other a 2,468cc model that evolved into a pure racing machine called the MKIII or Tigress. It wasn't an enormous success and was eclipsed by the smaller MG model.

MG also had successes in record breaking and in February 1931 a supercharged 743cc version of the engine was built and fitted to an experimental chassis. It became the smallest car in the world to achieve 100mph. It was good publicity for the launch two weeks later of the C-type Midget, an off-the-shelf production racer that was priced at only £295. The first 14 cars were delivered to Brooklands just in time for the Double Twelve-Hour Race, in which they took the first five places. MGs entered for Le Mans failed to achieve any podium finishes but other MG racers continued to collect silverware throughout the 1930s at Brooklands and elsewhere. One of the marque's greatest triumphs came in 1933 when a team of new supercharged 1,100cc K3 six-cylinder models were driven in the Mille Miglia and won their class and the team prize. MG cars continued to do what they did best – provide enthusiasts with affordable and competitive racing and sports machinery – up to and after the war.

M.G., 1931: Norman Black's 746-c.c. Supercharged '750 Montlhéry' Midget, winner of the 1931 Ulster Tourist Trophy Race.

Napier, 1903: S.F. Edge's 13-litre, 80 h.p. racer, depicted with bonnet removed, as
built for the 1903 Gordon Bennett Cup race.

NAPIER

Napier's last cars, delivered in 1925, were strictly luxury models, but a quarter
of a century earlier Napiers were serious racing machines. In 1900 Napier's
great salesman and protagonist Selwyn Francis Edge won a bronze medal in the
Thousand Miles Trial in his chain driven two-cylinder 8hp Napier. The same year
Edge entered a 4.9-litre four-cylinder machine producing 16hp in the
Paris–Toulouse–Paris race but retired. For the 1901 season Edge and Montague
Napier built a massive 17,157cc four-cylinder car that boasted 103hp, but at two
tons was far too heavy. The car was intended to compete in the Gordon Bennett
Trophy but was disqualified for having foreign-made tyres. For 1902 Edge and
Napier went back to the drawing board and came up with a lightweight machine
with a 6.5-litre engine that produced 45hp. This lighter approach did the trick and
Edge won the Gordon Bennett Cup. The next year's Gordon Bennett race, held in
Ireland, proved to be a fiasco for Napier. Edge himself finished last but was
disqualified for a push-start. The other team drivers Jarrott and Stocks both crashed
and withdrew from the race. Napier's last racing season was in 1908, by which time
the cars were more successful as record breakers and hillclimbers.

That wasn't the end of the Napier name in motor racing, though. The Napier
company also built aero-engines, and it was the advanced Napier Lion engine that
powered many land speed record cars in the 1920s and '30s, including Malcolm
Campbell's Bluebird and Sir Henry Segrave's Golden Arrow.

Vanwall, 1958: The Formula 1 Vanwall won the Grands Prix of Europe, Holland, Germany, Italy, Portugal and Morocco in 1958, securing the Manufacturers' Championship.

VANWALL

C.A. 'Tony' Vandervell ran a successful engine-bearing company. In 1950 his mechanics built a modified Ferrari named the 'Thinwall Special', in recognition of the trademark 'Thinwall' bearings used in its engine and for which the company was famous.

For the 1954 F1 season Vandervell decided to build his own cars. A 2.0-litre four cylinder engine was designed by an engineer called Leo Kuswicki, who worked for Norton motorcycles. The chassis was made by Cooper. The car was developed through 1954 and '55; the engine being enlarged to 2.2 litres and then 2.5 litres.

At the end of the 1955 season it was obvious that the engine was rather better than the chassis. Taking some good advice, Vandervell asked an up-and-coming designer called Colin Chapman (who was also running the fledgling Lotus operation) to come up with a new chassis. Chapman and aerodynamicist Frank Costin designed a new body incorporating a new five-speed gearbox fitted behind the fuel-injected 280bhp engine. The Vanwall was now a serious proposition. Vandervell hired Peter Collins, Mike Hawthorn and Ken Wharton to drive the cars, and then Stirling Moss, who started the trophy collection with victory in the 1956 Silverstone Daily Express Trophy.

The next year Moss had a successful year with three GP wins. But that was nothing compared to the 1958 season. At last a British team dominated Grand Prix racing. Moss and team mate Tony Brooks won three GPs apiece to give Vanwall the World Manufacturers' Championship. The team was disbanded at the end of the year on the advice of Vandervell's doctor, but the goal had been achieved.

CIRCUITS

Brands Hatch Circuit

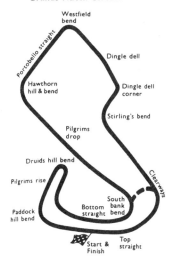

Brands Hatch

Set in rolling countryside in Kent's North Downs only 20 miles to the south east of London, Brands Hatch was actually used between the wars for motorcycle grass track racing but wasn't paved until it re-opened in 1949. Set in a natural bowl, the circuit is perfect for the spectator. The original kidney-shaped circuit was extended in 1954 with the addition of a loop up the hill to Druid's Hairpin. In 1960 the circuit was extended again to full grand prix length.

Crystal Palace

London's only motor racing circuit was built in the shadow of the Crystal Palace itself which sadly burnt down in 1936, the year before the circuit opened. In its original form the track was two miles long, but when racing returned to the Palace after the war in 1953, a new section of track was added that cut a corner to reduce the overall length. Because the circuit was near private housing only a few car and motorcycle meetings were held each year. It finally closed in 1974.

Crystal Palace Circuit

Goodwood

Goodwood circuit was one of Britain's first airfield circuits, laid out around the perimeter track of the old RAF Westhampnett fighter base. The 2.38-mile circuit sits at the bottom of the South Downs within sight of Chichester. The circuit was the brainchild of landowner the Duke of Richmond and Gordon, himself a keen flier and motorist. The first meeting was held on 18 September 1948 with Reg Parnell winning the Goodwood Trophy in his Maserati at 80.56mph.

Goodwood Circuit

Indianapolis Motor Speedway

The speedway at Indianapolis is the oldest racing circuit in the world that is still in use. It was built in 1909 and was first used for short races before in 1911 the first 500 mile race was held. The famous 'Indy 500' has been held every year since, apart from breaks during the two wars. The track was the brainchild of a local businessman called Carl G Fisher who, with partners, paid for construction of the 2.5-mile track. In its earlier days the track was paved with brick which gave Indianapolis its nickname 'The Brickyard'. The finishing line is still marked by a line of brick even though the rest of the circuit is paved in Tarmac.

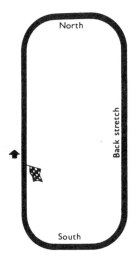

Le Mans

Races have been run on the public roads around the French town of Le Mans since 1906, when the first GP de l'ACF (Auto Club de France) was held there. However, it is as the venue for the famous 24 hour race that Le Mans is known around the world. The race was first held in 1923 on a 10.72 mile course that went from the start line into the suburbs of the town. The circuit was shortened by changes

in 1929 and has been modified many times since. The one famous section that has remained and is legendary in the world of speed, is the long Mulsanne straight which for 363 days of the year is Route Nationale 158.

Le Mans 24-Hour Race Circuit

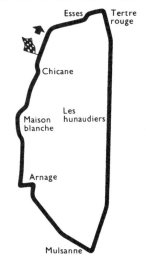

Mille Miglia

Inspired by France's Le Mans 24 hour race, a group of Italian enthusiasts decided to go one better and hold a race over a really long circuit. The result was the Mille Miglia or 'thousand miles', which was first held in 1927. The route started at Brescia and ran anti-clockwise down to Rome, returning northwards to Brescia and the finish. War interrupted the Mille Miglia but the great race was revived in 1947 with a new clockwise course that was 1,118.5 miles long. The race was dangerous, especially for spectators, and in 1957 two drivers and eleven spectators were killed in an accident. The mighty Mille Miglia lasted only one more year.

Mille Miglia Circuit

- ▬▬ Secondary paved roads
- ▭▭ Main roads
- ═══ Mountain passes and poor roads

Monaco

The famous Monaco street circuit was devised by Antony Noghes, president of the Monaco Car Club, in 1928 and first used the next year for the inaugural Monaco Grand Prix. The circuit is entirely made up from public roads and the layout of the 1.95-mile track has barely changed over the years. It is a unique circuit and now such a historical part of Grand Prix racing that it is inconceivable that it could be dropped from the calendar.

Monza Autodrome

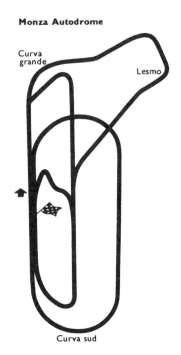

Autodromo dela Ciudad de Mexico

Monza

Monza is the home of Italian motor racing and attracts the most passionate of all racing's fans. The circuit lies in the attractive wooded grounds of the Monza royal park a mile or so north east of Milan. The original autodrome was built in 1922. Monza actually offered two circuits, one a 3.4-mile road course and the other a 2.79-mile banked track. The two could be combined to make a 6.21-mile course and was used in this form for the Italian Grand Prix from 1922-28 and from 1931-33. The Monza circuit is incredibly fast and in the 1930s various changes were made, including the addition of chicanes, to slow down the dominant 'Silver Arrows'.

Mexico

The Autodromo de la Ciudad de Mexico is an interesting venue for several reasons. Firstly, it is at an elevation of 7,500 ft, which significantly reduces engine power due to the thinner air. Second, the circuit is often in disrepair, with cracks in the Tarmac surface. Another issue is that crowd control has often been at best sporadic and at worst totally absent. The circuit was later renamed after local racing hero Ricardo Rodriquez who tragically died at the circuit during practice for the Mexican Grand Prix in the early 1960s.

Nürburgring

The building of the Nürburgring in the Eifel Mountains area to the west of the Rhine was a grand scheme proposed by the German government to not only bring jobs to the depressed area, but to provide a test track and racing venue for the national automotive industries. The result was the magnificent 17.563-mile circuit that opened in 1927. The track was made up of two sections: the Sudschleife (South Loop) and the Nordschleife (North Loop). The German Grand Prix was held at the track in 1927 and was fittingly won by a Mercedes-Benz. Crowds of up to 350,000 came to watch subsequent races, bringing substantial revenue to local businesses.

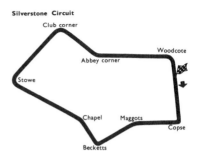

Silverstone Circuit

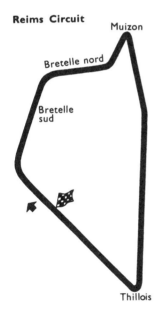

Reims Circuit

Reims

The Reims road course in the heart of Champagne country was first used in 1925. It is essentially triangular in shape and was extremely fast with some truly impressive lap times being posted. For example, in the 1939 Grand Prix de France, Hermann Müller, driving an Auto Union, raised the record for average lap speed to 105.249mph – and at that time the circuit included a section that passed through the village of Gueux! Long- distance sports car racing also took place on the circuit and in 1952 a curious feature was added: velvet curtains were hung from a purpose-built bridge beyond the hairpin to stop drivers from being dazzled by the early morning sun on the approach to Thillois.

Silverstone

Silverstone, established in 1948 on an old RAF bomber station, is a typical British airfield circuit: open, windy and very often bleak in the winter. It is, however, a tremendously exciting circuit with some very fast straights and equally quick corners. The first major meeting was the 1948 British Grand Prix, run on the 3.67 mile-long track that incorporated both main runways and sections of the perimeter road. Luigi Villoresi won the event in a Maserati at an average speed of 72.28mph. The next year the layout was changed, with cars only using the perimeter track.

Spa-Francorchamps Circuit

Spa-Francorchamps

Even the bravest of drivers face Belgium's challenging Spa circuit with trepidation. In 1924 a circuit was devised that linked the villages of Francorchamps, Malmedy and Stavelot forming a rough triangle. The wooded hills of the Ardennes are famed for their damp and unpredictable climate and many a driver has had to face the added challenge of a downpour or reduced visibility. The

first true Belgian GP was won by Antonio Ascari in an Alfa Romeo in 1925 at an average speed of 74.56mph. Sadly the Spa circuit has taken its toll on the ranks of racing drivers over the years, in 1939 claiming the life of Richard Seaman.

Targa Florio

The Targa Florio was one of the earliest motor races and is one of the most long-lived. For its early years, dating from the inaugural 1906 race, it was held on the mountain roads in Sicily that surround the capital Palermo using the 92.48 mile route of the 'Great' Madonie circuit. From 1919–1930 the 67.11 mile 'Medium' Madonie was used and then two years later the 'Short' Madonie. Whatever the length, the Targa Florio presented one of racing's greatest challenges. The event is more than a race, however, as the Sicilian locals come out in force with picnics and wine to watch international stars and local heroes race at crazy speeds through their villages and over the mountain roads.

Targo Florio

AUTO-UNION

ALFA-ROMEO

PLAYER'S CIGARETTES

E.R.A. 1½-LITRE

PLAYER'S CIGARETTES

MERCÉDÈS-BENZ